Styling the Post Office

John Chenery

An electric Royal Mail van, pillar box, and K2 telephone kiosk at Mount Pleasant © J. Chenery (2019).

A Light Straw publication 2022
Exploring Communications History

My GPO Family of Books [mygpofamily.com]

Other photobooks by the Author: *Poetry in the Post Office* (2019); *London's GPO Heritage* (2019); *The GPO and Bletchley Park (2020).*

GPO2 Mobile Post Office
Use of the MacDonald Gill designed monogram on mobile post office, registration GPO2 passing along Fleet Street (London) in the Lord Mayor's parade of 13 November 2010. GPO2 entered service in April 1938 as a mobile post office offering a counter service, public telephones, and telegram facilities.

John from the Postal History Society (PHS) dressed in an authentic Post Office uniform led members of the British Postal Museum & Archive (now The Postal Museum) and PHS in the parade © David Whittaker (2010).

Copyright

"Every effort has been made to trace and acknowledge all copyright holders, but if any have been inadvertently overlooked the author will be pleased to make the necessary acknowledgements at the first opportunity."

The words and images in this book are not intended to imply any endorsement from trading units of British Telecommunications plc., Openreach Ltd., International Distributions Services plc. (previously Royal Mail plc.), Post Office Ltd., NS & I, or any of their associated or derived companies. All logos, trademarks, brand names and images are the property of their respective owners and are used for review only.

All rights reserved. This book or any portion thereof may not be reproduced or used in any manner whatsoever without the express written permission of the author except for the use of brief quotations in a book review or scholarly journal. Although every precaution has been taken in the preparation of this book, the publisher and author assume no responsibility for errors or omissions.

The logos, designs, and lettering within have been scanned, photographed, or downloaded, and resized to fit these pages, for illustration purposes only. Lettering sizes, angles of photography etc., may have distorted the views. They are not suitable nor intended to be copied or reproduced elsewhere, nor to serve as a colour-matching reference. Colours of reproduction are not guaranteed to be accurate to the original specifications. Note that fading, copying and final printing may also have changed the colour tones.

Copyright © 2022 John Chenery

ISBN 978-1-8382940-1-4

First edition November 2022

A *Light Straw* publication LightStraw.co.uk formatted at *Fynevue* in England.
Printed in Great Britain by *Book Printing UK*. bookprintinguk.com

Introduction to Styling the Post Office

As with any business, the style of the Post Office affected how its staff and customers perceived and interacted with it. This book takes a snapshot of how just some of the associated key brands evolved through its long history to what they are today. Thousands of files have been 'crunched' in this quest to present a simplistic guide which could form the basis for further detailed study. Logos, symbols, designs, colours, and trademarks are featured here solely to demonstrate use of the brands, and copyright remains with the original creators, or subsequent assignee(s). This first edition covers an expansive timeline of changes, which I hope you will enjoy reading.

John Chenery
September 2022

Overview

Up until October 1969, the *Post Office* was the *GPO*; not that many people understood what it really meant, or how it was organised. The iconic red letter boxes, telephone kiosks, and delivery vans were all part of this image. And the post office was where everyone went to buy stamps or deposit money into the *Savings Bank*. *GPO Telephones* (sic) looked after those green cabinets on the street or whose engineer climbed a pole when you went 'on the telephone.' As a government department operating '*On Her Majesty's Service,*' the Post Office's associations with the Monarchy allowed it to display the Royal Cypher and Crown in various combinations throughout its organisation. And due to the fickleness of nationalities, different crowns and insignia treatments were later deemed essential for England, Scotland, and Wales.

With the freedom of corporation status from 1 October 1969, the Post Office sought to update its image into a coherent, co-ordinated business that both its staff and the public would comprehend. Re-styling the Post Office wasn't an easy task. Tradition, history, and public opinion weighed heavy, as did the sheer hierarchical challenges of agreeing new policies in short timescales. Designers *Banks and Miles* created a brand for the Post Office based upon a *Double Line* alphabet, the remnants of which remain with Royal Mail today. They also devised the dot-dash typeface for British Telecom.

The postal and telecommunications businesses have had their corporate identities refreshed many times since then as they strive to keep their company messages in focus and relevant to the products and services which they offer. Each brand seeks differentiation in the marketplace; this book aims to make sense of it all.

Contents

Copyright iii

Introduction iv

1: Origins of the General Post Office 1

2: The Men from the Ministries 11

3: Fonts and Foibles 19

4: Styling the Post Office 29

5.1: Brighter Post Offices 41

5.2: Building with Economy 49

5.3: South Molton 55

5.4: Knightsbridge 59

5.5: Ludgate Circus 63

5.6: Trafalgar Square 67

5.7: House Style 73

6.1: Saga of Postal Services Red 79

6.2: Telephone Kiosks 93

6.3: Post Office Red 101

7: Mid-Bronze Green 111

8: Towards Corporation Status 127

9: Safety Yellow 133

10.1: Banks and Miles 137

10.2: Banks and Miles - Postal 145

10.3: Banks and Miles - Telecommunications 149

11: British Telecom 153

12.1: Post Office Railway 161
12.2: Mail by Rail 167
13: Royal Mail '90 183
14.1: The Post Office 191
14.2: Consignia 193
15: Post Office Counters 195
16: BT '91 and Beyond 205
17: BT Comes Full Circle 217
18: Openreach 221
19: Post Office Tower 231
20: References and End Notes 235

Century Old Italic typefaces:
Keybridge House © Adam Oliver (2014).
Colombo House © J. Chenery (2019).
Fleet Building © J. Chenery (2006).

Lettering on telecommunication premises adopted various fonts.
During the BT '91 era, the style of *Century Old Italic* was favoured.
This was very similar to *Stempel Garamond Italic* which was used by Royal Mail.

1: Origins of the GPO

The transporting of the monarch's post, the royal mail dates back to 1516. However, it wasn't until regular stagecoaches were in use from about 1784, that the term *Royal Mail* was first seen as a brand name for the service. The General (letter) Post Office for commoners was consolidated in 1660 and since then the terms *General Post Office (GPO),* and *Royal Mail* became synonymous with the posting and delivery of letters. The development of the telegraph and telephone occurred during the period when the GPO as a company was responsible for both posts and telecommunications. This chapter aims to define and clarify the progression of the organisations and their identities.

The origin of the postal service dates to the time of Sir Brian Tuke, first Master of the Posts in 1516.

Mail coaches evolved to have red wheels, and together with the red uniform of the guard, and (later) red letter boxes, all contributed, albeit somewhat unintentionally to building a co-ordinated public image.

Mail coach and horses © Mark Skillen (2016). The guard, dressed in a red frock coat, is blowing the post horn to warn ahead of the mail coach's passage. As part of 'Royal Mail 500' (1516 to 2016) celebrations the mail coach was enroute to London's Guildhall on 18 June 2016.

Styling the Post Office

The King's ROYAL MAIL

The king's royal mail carried by horse-backed messengers circa 1516 eventually led to regular mail coach runs, and from about 1784 the name *Royal Mail* was first associated with the service.

The Post Office (Act 1635)

The setting-up of the first *public* postal service by Thomas Witherings in 1635 basically allowed the royal mail service (at least in name) to be used by commoners.

GENERAL POST OFFICE (GPO)

The Post Office (Act 1660)

Cromwell's 1657 act of *'Settling the Post'* in England, Scotland and Ireland which sought to formalise the service was disputed by Charles II. And thus, the Post Office act of 1660 was subsequently required to legally recognise the formation of the organisation, hence *'An Act for Erecting and Establishing a Post Office.'* The first Postmaster-General, Henry Bishop was appointed in 1660.

The act cites the setting up of 'one General Post Office.' It is conjectured that the use of the word 'General' was to imply the handling of all types of letter services, but nonetheless the name of the twentieth century company the *General Post Office* appears to originate from this act.

Royal Mail Brand

From 1660 until 1986, *Royal Mail* was simply a *brand* name of the letter-carrier service that was operated by the organisation named as the *General Post Office.*

The carriage of post by *Royal Mail*, and *'On His/Her Majesty's Service'* are words that evoke the impression of importance and expeditious delivery.

Page opposite: A simplified organisational progression of Royal Mail brand beginnings in 1516, through to the monopoly provider of the General Post Office in 1912, and thence to the 21st century splitting of companies.

Origins of the GPO

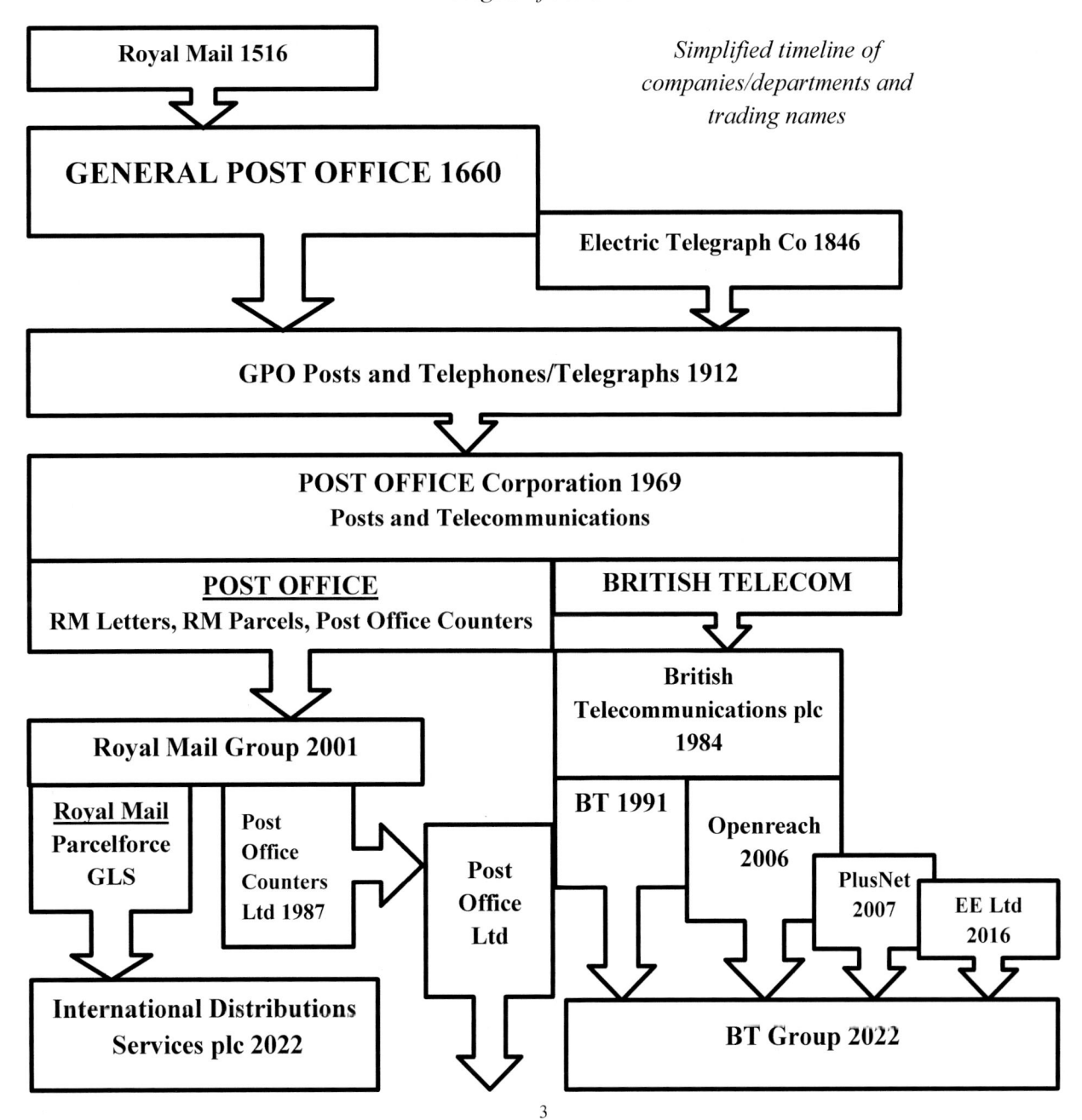

Simplified timeline of companies/departments and trading names

```
Royal Mail 1516
      ↓
GENERAL POST OFFICE 1660          Electric Telegraph Co 1846
              ↓                              ↓
      GPO Posts and Telephones/Telegraphs 1912
                        ↓
          POST OFFICE Corporation 1969
             Posts and Telecommunications
        ┌──────────────────┬──────────────────┐
     POST OFFICE                    BRITISH TELECOM
  RM Letters, RM Parcels,                  ↓
   Post Office Counters          British Telecommunications plc 1984
           ↓                              BT 1991
  Royal Mail Group 2001                    ↓        Openreach 2006
  ┌─────────────┬────────┐                                    PlusNet 2007   EE Ltd 2016
  Royal Mail    Post
  Parcelforce   Office         Post Office Ltd
  GLS           Counters
                Ltd 1987
       ↓                                    ↓
  International Distributions              BT Group 2022
  Services plc 2022
```

3

Styling the Post Office

TELECOMMUNICATIONS TIMELINE:

Electric Telegraph Company
The *Electric Telegraph Company* of 1846 is recorded as the origin of *British Telecommunications plc (BT)*.

GENERAL POST OFFICE

Telegraphs
Within the General Post Office, the Telegraph Acts of 1868-70 gave Her Majesty's Postmaster-General the right to acquire and operate the existing inland telegraph systems in the UK.

Post Office Telephones
From 1 January 1912 the General Post Office became the monopoly supplier of telephone services with the exception of the remaining municipal services in Hull, Portsmouth and Guernsey.

Thus, from 1912 the General Post Office was the single company responsible for both postal and telecommunication services in the UK.

POST OFFICE CORPORATION

On 1 October 1969, the Post Office became a public corporation/nationalised industry and was no longer a government department.

British Telecom-part of the Post Office
Progressively from c1970 Post Office Telephones styled itself as Post Office Telecommunications, then as a precursor to privatisation unveiled the new name of British Telecom in May 1980.

BRITISH TELECOMMUNICATIONS PLC

British Telecom remained the trading name as the separate British Telecommunications corporation was vested on 1 October 1981.
British Telecommunications plc was floated on the stock market on 6 August 1984.

BT became the new (simplified) trading name for British Telecommunications plc on 2 April 1991.

Origins of the GPO

OPENREACH

Openreach was created as a separate division of BT on 11 January 2006 manage the 'final-mile' copper network for Local Loop Unbundling (LLU) and effective competition in the marketplace.

Openreach Ltd was incorporated as a separate company, on 24 March 2017, owned by the BT Group. In July, the new branding was announced. The demarcation from BT was to satisfy the regulator OFCOM that Openreach would treat all Service Providers equally. Updated branding excluded any reference to BT as the parent company.

POSTAL TIMELINE:

POST OFFICE CORPORATION
Within the Post Office corporation formed in 1969, three business units were established in October 1986:

Royal Mail Letters, handling the mail.
Post Office Counters serving the public at post offices.
Royal Mail Parcels, handling bulkier packets.

Post Office Counters became Post Office Counters Ltd on 1 September 1987.

Parcelforce became the trading name of Royal Mail Parcels in August 1990. **Parcelforce Worldwide** was the extended name from 1997.

CONSIGNIA plc

With the Postal Services Act 2000, the Post Office corporation became a public limited company on 26 March 2001 and was renamed Consignia plc. Ownership remained with the Crown. At this point the long-established name Post Office, as the parent company, was swept away.

The new name was one of several options promulgated by consultancy firm Dragon Brands and was introduced by the Post Office's chief executive John Roberts on 9 January 2001 as *"modern, meaningful and entirely appropriate."*

ROYAL MAIL Group plc

Subsequently, Royal Mail as a top-level legal entity was created on 4 November 2002 because, in use the name Consignia was so unpopular.
The Independent newspaper wrote (23/05/2002) *"Consignia is to rename itself Royal Mail plc, reversing one of the most disastrous corporate re-brandings ever undertaken."*

The trading names remained as **Royal Mail** (for letters division) and **Parcelforce** (for parcels).
Exceptionally, in March 2002, the universal parcels service was transferred to Royal Mail leaving Parcelforce to concentrate on time guaranteed, next day and two-day express deliveries.

On 1 January 2006, slightly earlier than planned, Royal Mail lost its 350-year monopoly (thought to refer to *Settling the Post* act of 1657, thus 1657 to 2007), and the British postal market became fully open to competition.
During the move from government to private ownership several companies were set-up to facilitate the transition, namely: Royal Mail Holdings plc, Postal Services Holding Company, Royal Mail Group plc, Royal Mail Ltd.

On 20 March 2007 Royal Mail Group plc was re-registered as Royal Mail Group Ltd.
Royal Mail was floated on the Stock Market as Royal Mail plc on 15 October 2013. The government's remaining shares were sold on 12 October 2015. The holding company Royal Mail plc was renamed International Distributions Services plc on 3 October 2022.

POST OFFICE Ltd [counters business]

Within Consignia and later Royal Mail Group, Post Office Ltd (previously Post Office Counters Ltd 1987-2001) was a wholly owned subsidiary of the parent.

On 1 April 2012, Post Office Limited (POL) was demerged from Royal Mail Group and now reports directly to the Government. This is the only part of the original Post Office of 1660 which has not been privatised. Consequently a 10-year inter-business agreement (2012-2022) was signed between Royal Mail and POL to allow post offices to continue issuing stamps and handling letters and parcels for Royal Mail. A new Royal Mail/Post Office deal commenced on 29 March 2021 and is expected to operate at least until 28 March 2032.

ANNIVERSARIES

Royal Mail 500
Royal Mail celebrated its 500-year [1516 to 2016] anniversary in 2016. Royal Mail continues to be the *brand* of the Universal Service Obligation (USO) letter carrier, although between 1635 and 2001 the organisation was the responsibility of the Post Office.

Postal Service 300
The **General Post Office** celebrated its tercentenary [1635 to 1935] of the setting up of the first public postal service by Thomas Witherings on 31st July 1635.

GPO Tercentenary Greetings Telegram (1935)

TO THE POSTMASTER GENERAL

ON JULY 31ST THE BRITISH POST OFFICE WILL CELEBRATE ITS 300TH ANNIVERSARY, AND IT GIVES ME MUCH PLEASURE, IN THIS JUBILEE YEAR, TO SEND A MESSAGE OF CONGRATULATION AND GOOD WISHES TO THE MANY THOUSANDS OF ALL RANKS IN THE POST OFFICE SERVICE.

EVERY HOUSEHOLD IS MADE DAILY AWARE OF THE EFFICIENCY OF THEIR WORK WHICH IS CARRIED OUT WITH A PUNCTUALITY AND A CHEERFULNESS THAT COMMANDS THE ADMIRATION AND GRATITUDE OF THE PUBLIC.

ALTHOUGH MARKED PROGRESS HAS RECENTLY BEEN MADE, I FEEL SURE THAT THE NEXT FEW YEARS WILL WITNESS STILL FURTHER IMPROVEMENTS DESIGNED TO MEET THE REQUIREMENTS OF THE MILLIONS TO WHOM THE POST OFFICE SERVICE MEANS SO MUCH.

BUCKINGHAM PALACE GEORGE R.I.

BANKING TIMELINE:

Post Office Savings Bank (1861)

National Savings (1969)
NS and I (2002)

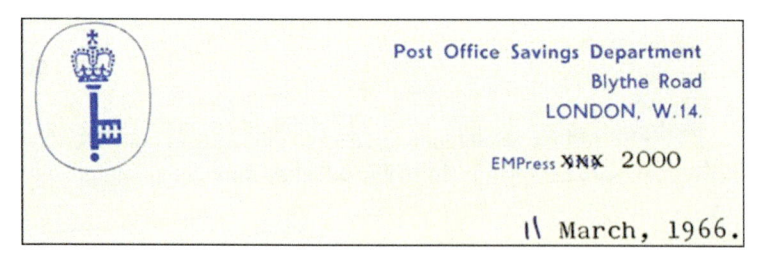

National Giro (1968)
National Giro (1972) separate business under PO Corporation
National Girobank (1978)
sold to Alliance & Leicester (1990)

POST OFFICE SAVINGS BANK (1861)
Founded within the Post Office to incentivise the public to save and accrue funds, in a secure place, that supported the nation (government).
Products included savings bonds, deposit accounts, and famously in 1956 **ERNIE** the Electronic Random Number Indicator Equipment which ran the Premium Bond prize draws.

DEPARTMENT FOR NATIONAL SAVINGS (1968)
The POSB became the Department for National Savings (DNS) on 1 April 1968.

NATIONAL SAVINGS BANK (1969)
Upon the Post Office gaining corporation status in 1969, the DNS transferred to the exchequer. By 2002 its name of National Savings & Investments, which reflected a wide portfolio of attractive rates, was abbreviated to **NS & I**.

NATIONAL GIRO (1968)
As a new Post Office department, National Giro was established as banking for the common man. In 1972 National Giro became a separate business within the newly formed Post Office corporation.

Under the Post Office corporation, it expanded to become **National Girobank** (1978) but was sold off to **Alliance & Leicester** (1990) and finally bought out by **Santander** in 2008.

Origins of the GPO

```
┌─────────────────────────────────────────────┐
│        GENERAL POST OFFICE 1660             │
└─────────────────────────────────────────────┘
                      ↓
┌─────────────────────────────────────────────┐
│              GPO Departments                │
├──────────────┬──────────────────┬───────────┤
│   National   │ Telephones/Tele- │Post Office│
│   Giro 1968  │ graphs and       │Savings    │
│              │ Postal 1912      │Bank 1861  │
└──────────────┴──────────────────┴───────────┘
       ↓              ↓                 ↓
┌──────────────────────────────┐   ┌──────────┐
│ POST OFFICE Corporation 1969 │   │National  │      ┌────────┐
│ Posts and Telecommunications │   │Savings   │  →   │NS and I│
│      & National Giro         │   │Bank 1969 │      │ 2002   │
└──────────────────────────────┘   └──────────┘      └────────┘
           ↓                                              ↓
    National Giro 1972
           ↓
┌──────────┐    ┌────────────┐    ┌──────────────┐
│National  │ →  │Alliance &  │ →  │Santander 2008│
│Girobank  │    │Leicester   │    │              │
│ 1978     │    │ 1990       │    │              │
└──────────┘    └────────────┘    └──────────────┘
```

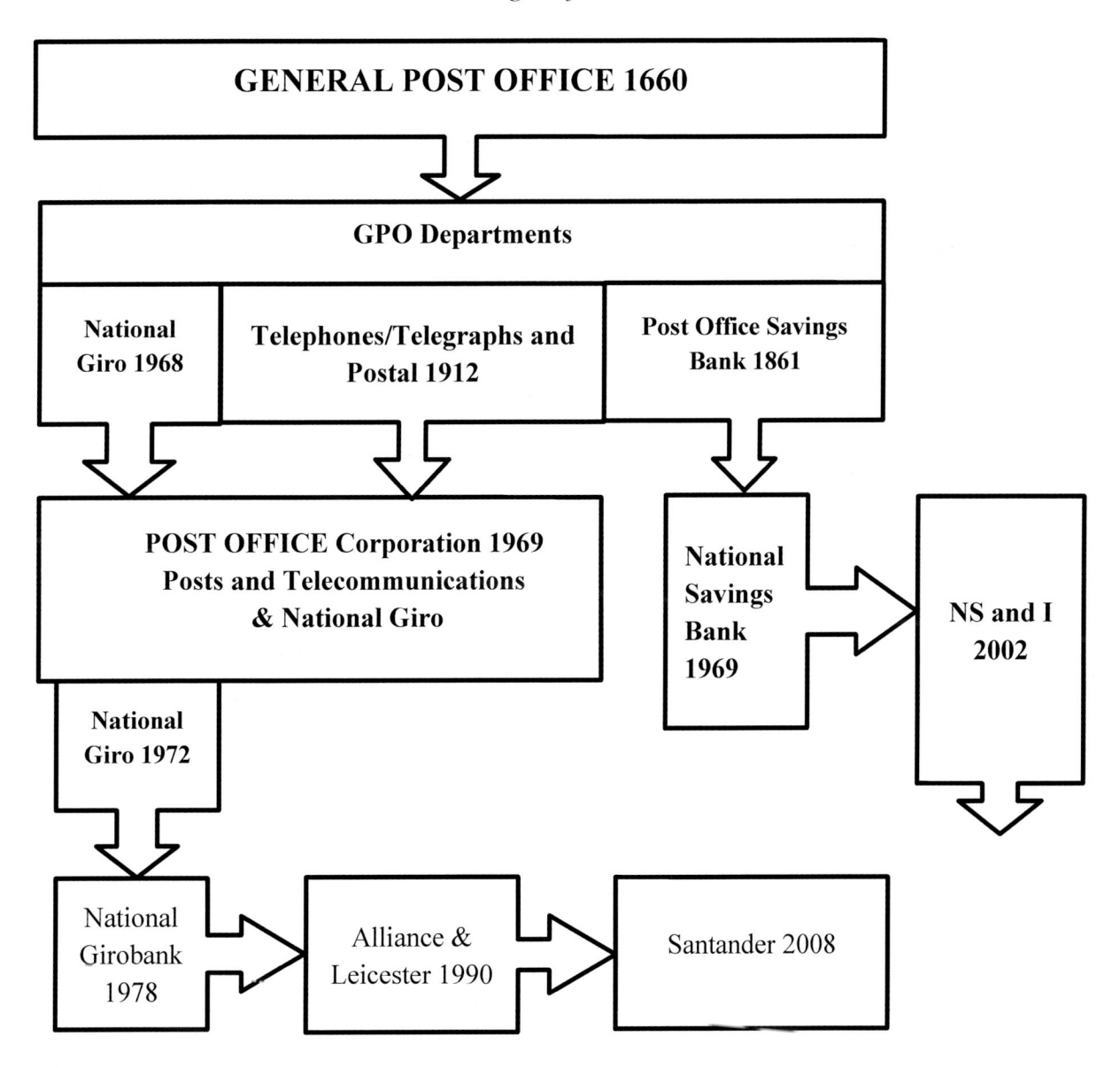

Simplified timeline of banking companies within the Post Office organisation

Styling the Post Office

ANNIVERSARIES cont'd

Letter Office 300 and Postal Service 350

In 1960 the GPO celebrated the tercentenary of Charles II's act of establishing a General Letter Office (post office) 1660 to 1960.
In 1985, Royal Mail celebrated 350 years of the public postal service that was established in 1635.

Left: Ideal Home Exhibition 1-26 March 1960. Image courtesy of BT Group Archives. Ref: TCB 473/P 7253.
Right: Postcard scan 'Royal Mail 350 years of service to the public.'

Queen Elizabeth II (Reign 1952 to 2022) and King Charles III Proclamation

Whereas it has pleased Almighty God to call to His Mercy our late Sovereign Lady Queen Elizabeth the Second of Blessed and Glorious Memory, by whose Decease the Crown of the United Kingdom of Great Britain and Northern Ireland is solely and rightfully come to The Prince Charles Philip Arthur George: We, therefore, the Lords Spiritual and Temporal of this Realm and Members of the House of Commons, together with other members of Her late Majesty's Privy Council and representatives of the Realms and Territories, Aldermen and Citizens of London, and others, do now hereby with one voice and Consent of Tongue and Heart publish and proclaim that The Prince Charles Philip Arthur George is now, by the Death of our late Sovereign of Happy Memory, become our only lawful and rightful Liege Lord Charles the Third, by the Grace of God of the United Kingdom of Great Britain and Northern Ireland and of His other Realms and Territories, King, Head of the Commonwealth, Defender of the Faith, to whom we do acknowledge all Faith and Obedience with humble Affection; beseeching God by whom Kings and Queens do reign to bless His Majesty with long and happy Years to reign over us. Given at St. James's Palace this tenth day of September in the year of Our Lord twenty thousand and twenty-two.

    God Save The King.

The next chapter outlines the people and organisations that were to shape the business direction and style(s) of the General Post Office and its departments.

2: Men from the Ministries

...and other establishments

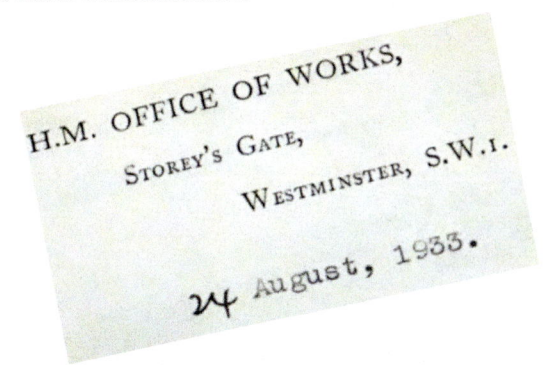

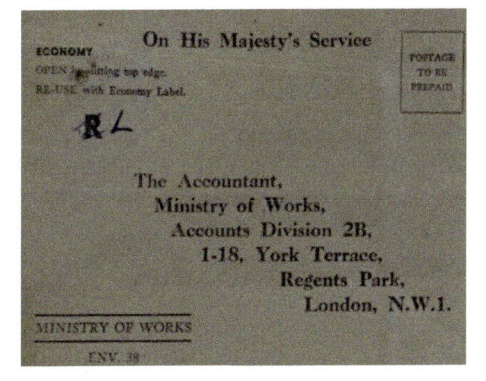

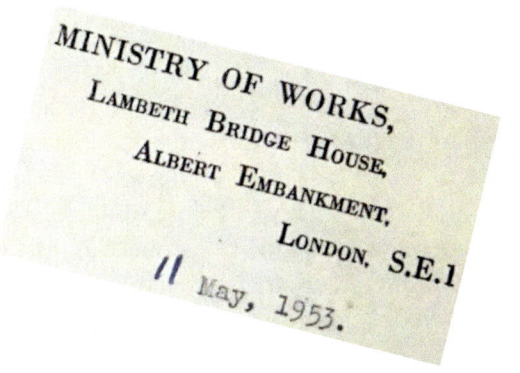

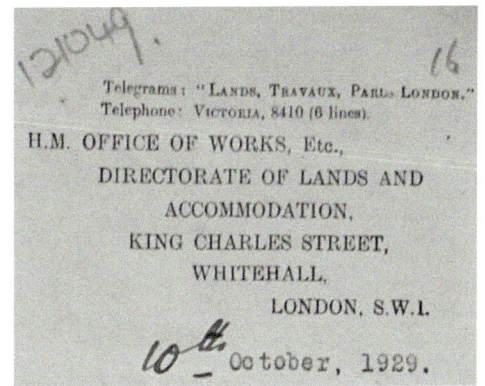

The Post Office's image was somewhat influenced by the practicalities of serving the public, but mostly by 'the men from the ministries' such as the Ministry of Public Building & Works (MPB & W), the Empire Marketing Board, and other public bodies, such as the Council of Industrial Design (CoID), and the Royal Fine Art Commission.

As the decades progressed, external agencies commanded greater influence over corporate design matters. This chapter also touches on the evolving branding, and identities of other key utilities as the need to be recognisably unique and coordinated became a necessity.

Styling the Post Office

The Office of Works
This existed as long ago as 1378 with a duty for the Royal Estate, buildings, and residences of the king. From about 1851 the Office was responsible to Parliament.

World War II established an urgent need for new government office and utility buildings, and so the Ministry of Works and Buildings was formed in 1940. The department went through many changes of title as its remit altered over the years:

- 1940 to 1942 Ministry of Works and Buildings
- 1942 to 1943 Ministry of Works and Planning
- 1943 to 1962 Ministry of Works
- 1962 to 1970 Ministry of Public Building and Works
- 1970 became part of the Department of the Environment
- 1972 most functions transferred to PSA (Property Services Agency)
- Early 1990s splitting up of PSA and privatisation of services

George Mansell, lecturer at the London County Council (Putney) School of Art:

"Where H.M. Office of Works are concerned there is a much higher standard of [lettering] work. The Office of Works should busy itself in the affairs of any Government Ministry that had set about making signs."

As part of the government and crown, GPO buildings were designed by architects from the Ministry of Works. A few notable architects and buildings are:

Henry Tanner: Post Office Savings Bank, Carter Lane (1890–94) and Post Office Savings Bank HQ, Blythe House (1899).

Albert Robert Myers: Faraday Building/International Telephone Exchange (1933)

WS Frost: Fleet Building/International Telex Exchange (1959)

Eric Bedford: Post Office Tower (1961-65); Faraday Building extension 1960s.

Royal Fine Art Commission (1924-1999)
The Commission was appointed by royal warrant in May 1924 to enquire into the artistic or otherwise suitability of schemes and amenities which were referred to it by government departments e.g., the Post Office. By 1946, its remit was wide-ranging and inevitably included the design of public telephone kiosks.

Men from the Ministries

Giles Gilbert Scott (1880-1960)
Architectural designer of Bankside Power Station, Battersea Power Station, Liverpool Cathedral, Forth Road Bridge, Edinburgh, and others.
Scott designed the K2, K3 and K6 telephone kiosks for the Post Office.
K2 1924 cast iron
K3 1929 concrete
K4 adapted K2 by POED (Post Office Engineering Department)
K5 Post Office prototype
K6 1935 cast iron

Empire Marketing Board (1926)
Was formed in May 1926 by the Colonial Secretary Leo Amery to promote trade within the Empire. From 1927, this was aided by the EMB Film Unit, under the direction of Sir Stephen Tallents with John Grierson. Although the EMB was disbanded by 1933, Tallents transferred his ground-breaking documentary film unit to the GPO.

London Underground:

Edward Johnston (1872-1944)
In 1913, Frank Pick commissioned him to design a typeface for what was to later to become London Underground (LU)/TfL. The simple and clear sans-serif Johnston typeface was the result. From 1933 the iconic letters were also used on all versions of Harry Beck's famous underground map. The Johnston Sans typeface association with LU is one the most enduring examples corporate branding. In 1979 Johnston Sans was redesigned by Eiichi Kono at Banks & Miles (brand consultants) to become New Johnston, which was more suitable for phototypesetting in the evolving world of word processors and computers.
Johnston's student Eric Gill, who worked on the development of the original typeface, later used it as a model for his own Gill Sans.

Eric Gill (1882-1940)
Eric was a sculptor, and typeface designer.

His Gill Sans typeface (designed 1926-30) was based upon the sans-serif lettering of Johnston Sans (London Underground). Gill Sans was probably adopted more widely because its use wasn't restricted to LU only.

In 1928–29, Gill carved three of the eight relief sculptures on the theme of winds, for Charles Holden's headquarters for the London Electric Railway (now TfL) at 55 Broadway (St. James's Park tube station.)

Styling the Post Office

W H Smith (WHS)
Eric Gill's early work in 1903 included him signwriting (in person) the shop front of W H Smith on the Rue de Rivoli in Paris. This was the first of many fascia boards hand-lettered by Gill for W H Smith at the instigation of St John Hornby, a director of the company who was a great Arts
and Crafts patron, and connoisseur of lettering. From about 1907 W H Smith's own signwriters adopted the style and it continued as a corporate identity for many decades. [Reference: *Eric Gill: A Lover's Quest for Art and God* by Fiona MacCarthy.]

Finally in 1996 Colin Banks [of Banks & Miles] interpreted Eric Gill's signwriting style for Monotype and created *Gill Facia*, described as an elegant signage face for advertisements and displays.

MacDonald (Max) Gill (1884-1947) Brother of Eric Gill
Mapmaker, graphic designer, letterer, and architect who designed eight posters for the EMB and notably went on to devise the first GPO monogram in 1935. [Ref: https://macdonaldgill.com/]

The GPO Film Unit (1933)

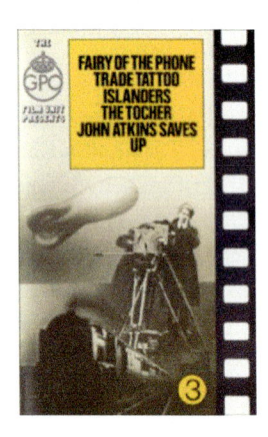

Producing well known classics such as *Night Mail* the *GPO Film Unit* was established in 1933. In 1940 it was renamed the *Crown Film Unit* following its transfer to the *Ministry of Information*.

Scan of VHS cover #3: Fairy of the Phone; Trade Tattoo; Islanders; The Tocher; John Atkins Saves Up.

Ministry of Information (1939)
From 1939 to 1945 the Ministry of Information was responsible for publicity and propaganda in aid of the war effort providing news and press censorship, both at home and abroad.

Men from the Ministries

Design Research Unit (1942)

DESIGN RESEARCH UNIT	
	MISHA BLACK OBE RDI FPSIA M INST RA
	MILNER GRAY RDI FPSIA
	Ronald Armstrong
ARCHITECTS AND DESIGNERS	Kenneth Bayes FRIBA MSIA
	Alexander Gibson FRIBA AA Dipl
	Kenneth Lamble MSIA
37 PARK STREET LONDON W1	Dorothy Goslett *Business Manager*
TELEPHONE MAYFAIR 9255 TELEGRAMS DRUNIT AUDLEY LONDON	

Misha Black
Milner Gray
Ronald Armstrong
Kenneth Bayes
Alexander Gibson
Kenneth Lamble
Dorothy Goslett

The DRU was founded by Herbert Read, Misha Black (1910-1977) and Milner Gray (1899–1997) and was the first consultancy to combine expertise in architecture, graphics, and industrial design. Other notable associates were Stuart Rose, and Sir Hugh Casson who were later to collaborate on projects for the GPO. In 2004, the DRU merged with Scott Brownrigg (architects) and persists at www.scottbrownrigg.com.

Of all the organisations, in partnerships with its associates, the DRU was to produce some of the most innovative and long-lasting corporate designs of the 20th century. Examples included designs for Imperial Chemical Industries (ICI), Ilford (photo), and outstandingly the British Rail Corporate Identity Manual (1965).

Council of Industrial Design (1944)
Was established with the aim '*to promote by all practicable means the improvement of design in the products of British industry.*' Known today as the Design Council www.designcouncil.org.uk.

Central Office of Information (1946)
On 1st April 1946 the Central Office of Information (COI) took over many of the responsibilities which were previously the remit of the Ministry of Information. Under the direction of departmental ministers and answerable to Parliament, the COI was concerned with overseas publicity, cultural, educational and trade operations. To promote long-term education, information films were part of the output of the Central Office of Information. John Grierson, previously of the GPO Film Unit, was Controller of Films at the Central Office of Information in London (1948-1950). In May 1972, the COI was placed under the control of the Civil Service. On 31 March 2012, the COI finally closed its doors.

German-born Heinrich Fritz Kohn spent some time designing posters for the Ministry of Information before setting up his own corporate design company: Henrion Design Associates.

Styling the Post Office

Henrion Design Associates (1951)
The founder, formally known as Frederick Henri Kay Henrion used his more familiar name of Henri Henrion (HH) in his business dealings.

Henrion Design Associates
Consultant Designers
35 Pond Street London NW3
Telephone HAMpstead 7897/7948

In early 1965, Henrion was invited to advise on, and assist in creating a new unified public identity for the General Post Office. Heavy with bureaucracy, the government-run organisation was not very receptive to external meddling and despite some novel ideas, Henrion's themes were not adopted.

Festival of Britain (3 May to 30 September 1951)
Was a special exhibition devised to showcase British innovation and design as the country recovered from the austerity of World War II. In a similar way of the London 2012 Olympic Park of the 21st century, the festival site on the south bank was envisaged to be redeveloped after the event, apart from the Royal Festival Hall which remains today.

Sir Hugh Casson was appointed director of the Festival of Britain, while Neville Conder assisted him with exhibition designs. Misha Black of the DRU coordinated the designs for the Dome of Discovery, the Regatta Restaurant, and the Bailey Bridge.

Associates of the DRU collaborated with other designers as well as forming external partnerships. Sir Hugh Casson teamed with Neville Conder (1922-2003) to form the Casson Conder Partnership in 1956.

Casson Conder Partnership (1956)

SIR HUGH CASSON & NEVILLE CONDER Architects

PARTNERS SIR HUGH CASSON RDI, MA, FRIBA, NEVILLE CONDER FRIBA, AA Dip. Hons., MSIA
ASSOCIATES MICHAEL CAIN ARIBA, AA Dip., R A GREEN ARIBA, AA Dip., TIMOTHY RENDLE ARIBA

35 Thurloe Place London SW7 KNIGHTSBRIDGE 4581

Men from the Ministries

In 1957 Conder submitted his design for a modern (aluminium) telephone kiosk (K7) to the Post Office. The concept was too ahead of its time in an era where red cast iron structures were still regarded as public icons and formed an integral part of the Post Office's identity. Prototype K7s were installed, but the design never went into production.

Transport

The stunning simplicity of a unified alphabet, *Johnston Sans* to direct passengers on London Underground was about to be usurped as road, rail and air transport literally took off and urgently needed its signage updating.

Britain's first motorway section, the M6 Preston Bypass, was to open in 1958 but the high-speed road required radically new signage for drivers to quickly and safely recognise their route between junction layouts and exits. The Anderson Committee of 1957 commissioned graphic designer Jock Kinneir to develop a complete scheme.

Jock Kinneir (1917-1994)

After teaching engraving, painting, and illustration at Chelsea College of Art, Jock Kinneir worked on exhibition design for the Central Office of Information. In 1950 he joined the DRU but left to establish his own design business in 1956. Jock's illustration design student Margaret Calvert was ideally suited to assist him. Their work together as **Kinneir Calvert Associates (1964)** on signage was to radically shape the everyday street scene across the whole of the UK.

Douglas Scott (1913–1990)

As an industrial designer, Scott was said to have been a '*master of the undulating curve*'!
His notable work was on all types of body casings ranging from the Aga cooker to the Routemaster bus. Circa 1958 he designed the Pay on Answer (POA) payphone (casing) which was used in telephone kiosks for Subscriber Trunk Dialling (STD) of telephone calls. In the 1960s he collaborated with Associated Automation in the production of self-service vending machines which became an integral feature of modernised post offices. Scott was appointed *Royal Designer for Industry* in 1974.

Hall Telephone Accessories (1921)

The integral coin-mechanism (payment system) for the POA payphone was devised and manufactured by the then established and renamed **Associated Automation** of Willesden, London. The company produced units for the GPO/Post Office Telecommunications until electronic processor systems made their mechanical work redundant.

Styling the Post Office

Martyn Rowlands (1923-2004)
At London's Central School of Art and Design, Douglas Scott taught industrial design to students such as Martyn Rowlands who went on to conceive the stylish *Trimphone* telephone for the GPO. Manufactured by STC (Standard Telephones and Cables), as the *Deltaphone*, the product won a *Design Council* award in 1966 and remained a style icon for many decades later.

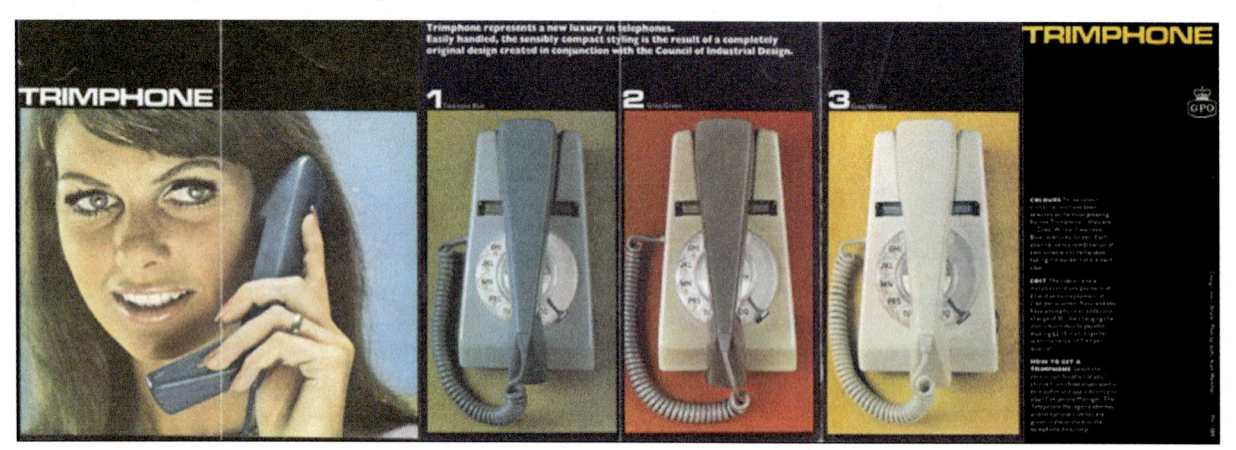

Above: Trimphone leaflet PH 1089 – Design John Ward; photography Alan Marshall. 'Trimphone represents a new luxury in telephones. Easily handled, the sensibly compact styling is the result of a completely original design created in conjunction with the Council of Industrial Design.' Colours: Two-tone Blue, Grey/Green, and Grey/White.

White Heat

The forthcoming *White Heat* technological era of the 1960s, also a time of great social change, was the catalyst for the foundation of many new and lasting public utility identities, which have become so integrated into our way of life that they are taken for granted. Their design application, so simple, and yet the result so profound. A co-ordinated brand for the Post Office had to wait until the end of the decade, when the business itself was restructured, but elsewhere the ever-more-busy commercial world had a need to be both well-organised and recognised, as never before.

Left: Photo of a new contemporary mural in Clipstone Mews © J. Chenery (August 2022).

3: Fonts and Foibles

Overview
The development of other public institutions' media is included in these pages both for comparison and to demonstrate the everlasting impact of well thought out design. Special fonts, typefaces, and custom-designed alphabets were all elements of corporate styling which helped to project a consistent identity.

Digital Media
Historically, typefaces were designed and produced for hot-metal printing rather than constituting an image from pixels on a computer screen. Companies with well-established, iconic branding had to adapt their presentations to suit screen-based media. This was a gradual change over the decades that computers became ever more popular. By the 2010s, the proliferation of smart mobile phones and tablets, together with high definition smart TVs, meant that digital media was the primary target for corporate awareness. Consequently, mainstream brands invested heavily to ensure their images stayed both on message and on screen! The BBC (British Broadcasting Corporation), over many years, changed its iconic three letters from slanting, to upright, to upright with more spacing (2021), much to the amusement of its licence-paying audiences. To maintain integrity in an ever changing world the best brands have evolved and re-invented themselves many times over.

Intro
The *Art Deco* movement (circa 1925) of stylish architecture began a golden age of design. It was becoming more important for organisations to have a co-ordinated image in order to effectively promote and advertise their products and services.

Andrew Emmerson writes, *"During the 1930s the Ministry of Public Buildings and Works designed a standard lettering style for use on government buildings which was based on Trajan's Column. This is generally called 'Ministry' lettering and was used for hand-painted signwriting and for metal letters on buildings."*

Styling the Post Office

Ministry of Works Trajan Letterset

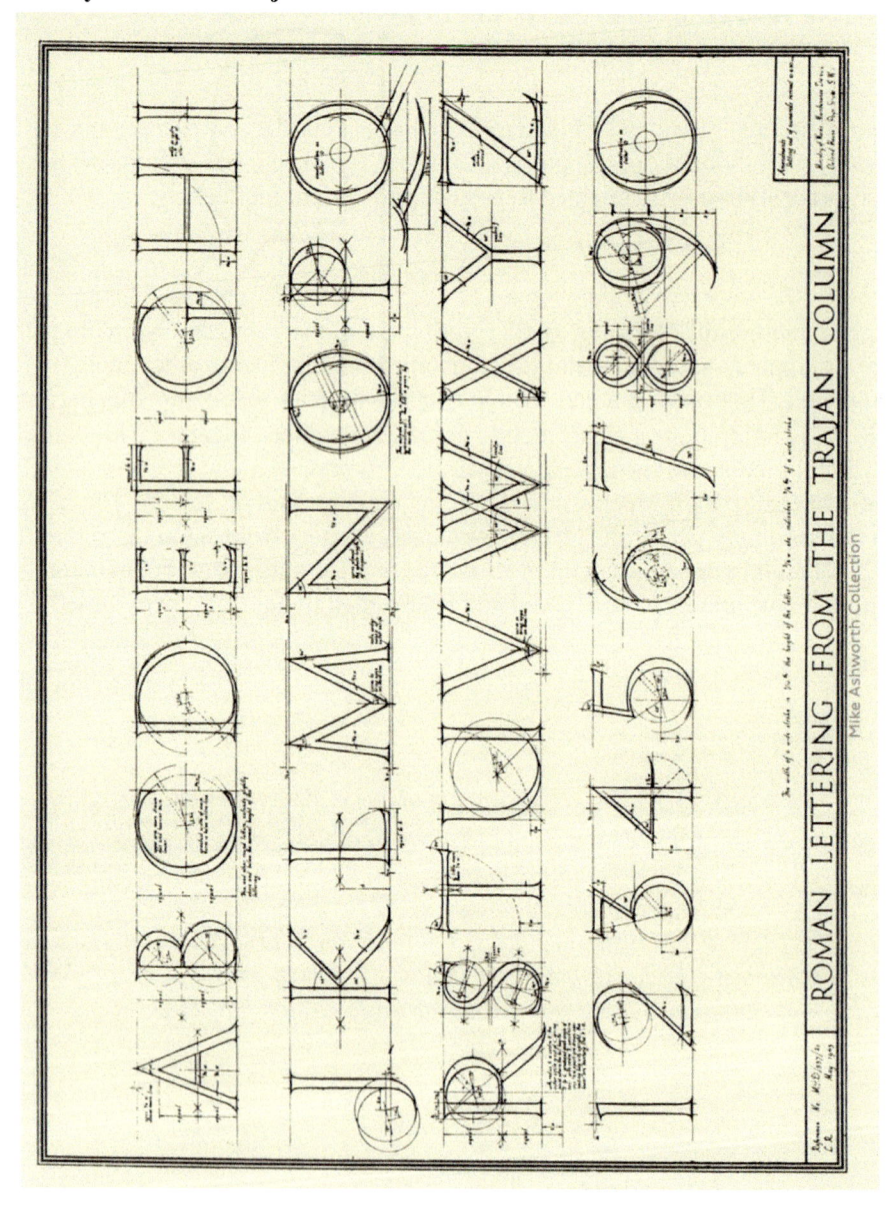

The Ministry of Works Trajan Roman lettering guide May 1945 Maintenance Division, Cleland House, Page Street, London, SW. Courtesy of the Mike Ashworth Collection.

Fonts and Foibles

Post Office Publications

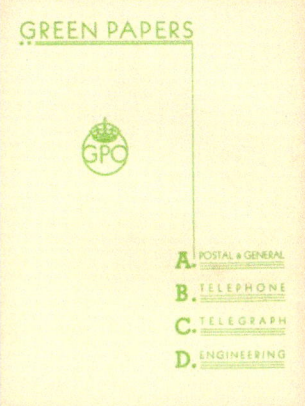

During the mid-1930s, the *Green Papers* series of Post Office educational pamphlets used a Kabel font, together with the Tudor crown GPO monogram.

Kabel is a geometric sans-serif typeface by the German designer Rudolf Koch and was released by the Klingspor foundry from 1927 onwards.

Gill Sans Shadow 338 designed by Eric Gill for Monotype in 1929.

A modern digitised version is named *K22 Eric Gill Shadow* (2011).

House journals of the 50s and 60s still hadn't developed a unified corporate style. *Right POTJ Winter 1960. Above POTJ Spring 1969.*

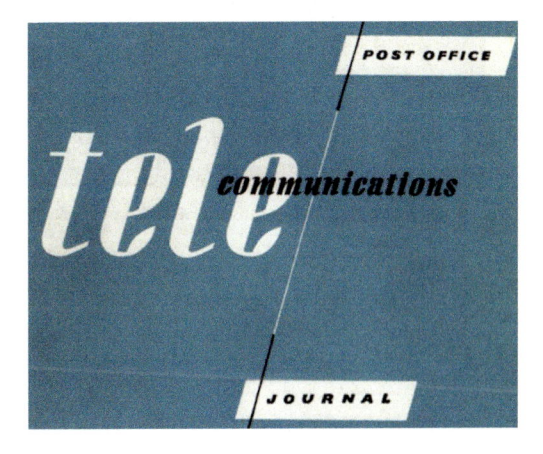

Styling the Post Office

London Underground

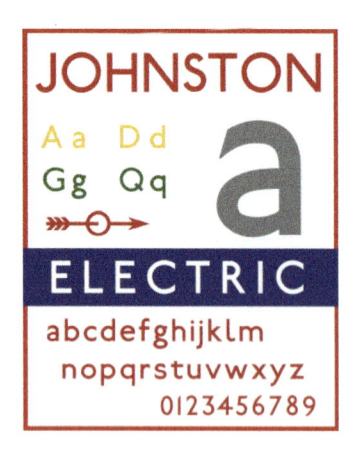

Somewhat ahead of the curve, in 1913 Frank Pick commissioned Edward Johnston to design a typeface for what was later to become London Underground (LU)/TfL. The simple and clear sans-serif Johnston typeface was the result.

Image from Wikipedia with Creative Commons license.

In 1979 Johnston Sans was redesigned by Eiichi Kono at *Banks and Miles* (brand consultants) to become *New Johnston*, which was more suitable for phototypesetting in the evolving world of word processors and computers.

Launched in July 2016 *Johnston100* was commissioned to cater for the expansion of London's transport system, from station maps to mobile apps. *Johnston100* was produced by the Monotype team which included Type Director Nadine Chahine, and Senior Type Designer Malou Verlomme.

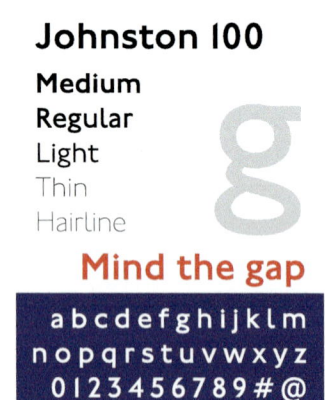

Johnston 100 (1915 to 2015) - A hundred years of typeface!

Johnston100 restores idiosyncrasies of Edward Johnston's original design, such as the distinctive diagonal bowl on the lowercase 'g'.

Johnston 100 was destined to be used for signing the new Crossrail *Elizabeth Line* as well as widespread use for new maps and posters. The *Elizabeth Line* was officially opened by Queen Elizabeth II on 17 May 2022.

Image from Wikipedia with Creative Commons license.

Fonts and Foibles

The Evolving Typeface of London Underground

"*Johnston is not just our typeface,*" Says Mike Ashworth, London Underground's Design and Heritage Manager, *"It is the very typeface of London. You will find no Londoner who does not recognise it, nor the simplicity and authority Johnston brings to this city."*

See Wikipedia for more details. Creative Commons Attribution-Share Alike 4.0 International license.

Gill Sans
Designed by Eric Gill.

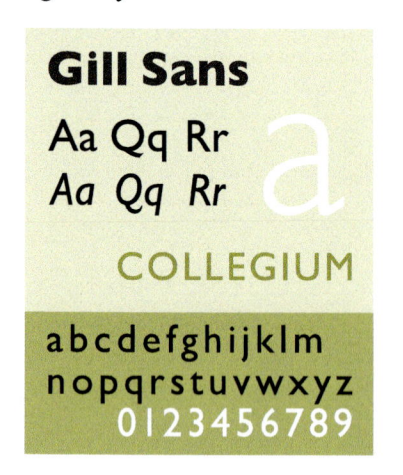

Gill Sans
Aa Qq Rr
Aa Qq Rr
COLLEGIUM
abcdefghijklm
nopqrstuvwxyz
0123456789

POST OFFICE
ROYAL MAIL
Office
GPO

Opposite: Specimen of the typeface Gill Sans by Jim Hood.

Alphabet image from Wikipedia with Creative Commons license.

LNER
The London North Eastern Railway (LNER) adopted Gill Sans (Monotype) throughout its organisation to produce a coherent corporate identity.

Use in the Post Office
The vehicle fleets of Royal Mail, and Post Office Telephones, showed no connection to each other, or to the parent department of the GPO, other than the Crown, although liveries and lettering were well-defined in each group.

For Post Office Telephones vans of the *Mid-Bronze Green* era the letterset was a derivation of Gill Sans. By comparison, the 'Os' appear particularly squashed.

Lettering on vehicle GYY 107 U39896 at Debden store © J. Chenery (2014).

In his book *GPO Design Posters,* Paul Rennie observes that the Post Office's use of typography was at times far from consistent in presenting a coordinated public image.

Fonts and Foibles

Transport, Rail, and Motorway

Kinneir Calvert Associates (1964)
As graphic designers, Jock Kinneir and Margaret Calvert notably worked on projects for Gatwick Airport, and the Department of Transport (DoT) at a time when both air and road travel was becoming popular with the masses, and there was an urgent need for clear signage to direct vehicles and passengers to their destinations.

Their specially created *Motorway* typeface was designed to be read from fast-moving vehicles with ease. Since the installation on the M6 Preston bypass was completed in 1958, their signage was (and is) used on all the UK's motorways.

The *Transport* typeface, developed between 1957 and 1963, was used for all other types of roads. Famously, Calvert designed the new pictorial road signs which included *Men at Work*, and *Schoolchildren nearby*.

Rail Alphabet

British Rail

In 1964 the Design Research Group (DRU) was commissioned to create a unified corporate identity for British Rail, which from 1965 was to be the trading name of British Railways.

Kinneir/Calvert adapted their *Transport* typeface to become the *Rail Alphabet*; yet another iconic brand that was to persist for many decades.

Alphabet image from Wikipedia with Creative Commons license.

Styling the Post Office

Clarendon
A slab-serif typeface released in 1845 by Thorowgood and Co. (or Thorowgood and Besley) of London, a letter foundry often known as the Fann Street Foundry.

Alphabet image from Wikipedia with Creative Commons license.

Clarendon was used on DLs (Descriptive Leaflets) up to the mid-1960s.

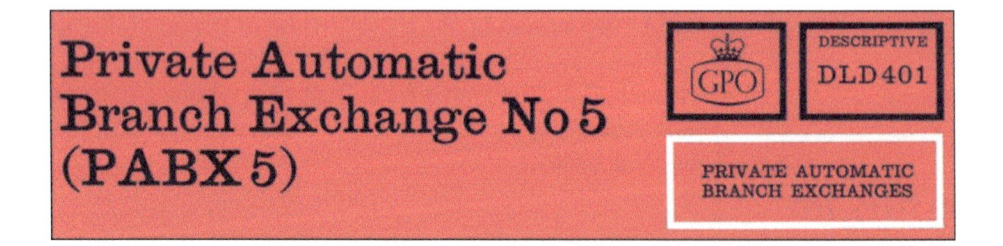

PABX5 leaflet DLD 401 1962, and Telex Service leaflet DLX-2 December 1963.

Clarendon

TELEPHONE EXCHANGE

Examples of Clarendon and Clarendon italic.

It was common practice to include the Royal Cypher, and the build date, on public service premises. As the Post Office was a government department this also included its telephone exchanges. The full lettering *TELEPHONE EXCHANGE,* in Clarendon font, was particularly noticeable during the 1950s and 60s which were a time of expansion and new building in the telephone service. After October 1969 the changed status of the Post Office dictated that its association with the Crown was lessened, and new commercial branding gradually took over.

Post Office Act 1969

"It is hereby declared that the Post Office is not to be regarded as the servant or agent of the Crown, or as enjoying any status, immunity or privilege of the Crown, or (subject to the express provisions of this Act relating to stamp duty) as exempt from any tax, duty, rate, levy or other charge whatsoever, whether general or local, and that its property is not to be regarded as property of, or property held on behalf of, the Crown."

Styling the Post Office

Cheltenham

Cheltenham was a Serif typeface released in 1903.
Left: An example of ITC Cheltenham typeface (1975). Image from Wikipedia with Creative Commons license.

From October 1969 the logo/typeface transitioned from GPO Telephones/Post Office Telephones to Post Office Telecommunications and it took a while to settle on a Cheltenham styled font (below centre and right) for the department's name on printed advertising media. Note: The 'O' appears slightly fatter in the examples than the standard font.

DLE 531
February 1970
Telephone Apparatus
POST OFFICE
TELECOMMUNICATIONS

DLC 1
October 1970
Index and Charges Section C leaflets
Post Office Telecommunications

The Ideal Phone. Stand 203.
Post Office Telecommunications

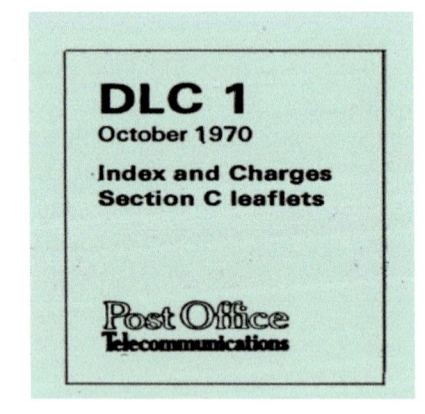

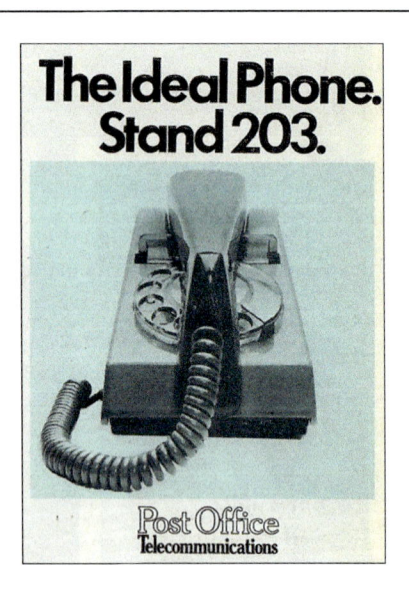

Far right: Advert for Post Office Telecommunications (stand 203) at the Ideal Home Exhibition (1972).

Used for Post Office Telecommunications from about 1970 until the *Banks and Miles* double line alphabet was phased in from 1974.

4: Styling the Post Office

GPO

The definitive name for the General Post Office was never particularly clear. Tracing the common usage, even in the twentieth century often defied logic. Regardless of the official name for a business entity, the public would frequently adopt a more familiar name, sometimes through lack of knowledge of the company structure, and long after the brand may have evolved.

The public visited a post office to buy stamps and send a letter, which was delivered by Royal Mail, and somehow the GPO was responsible for it all?

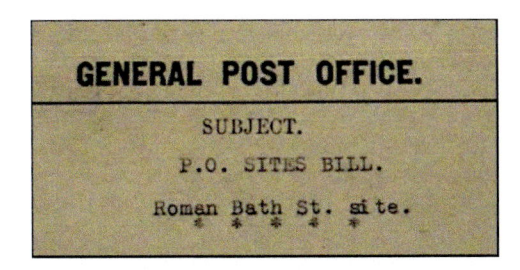

For internal correspondence, the individual page marking **GPO** often was used. Another example from 1934 shows the full text **GENERAL POST OFFICE** on a folder front, which then contradicts the term by also using **P.O.** on the line below.

Realistically, the above example was in fact historical papers catalogued in a more modern folder, but the contradiction in naming invariably persisted.

This perception was not helped by the fact that post offices were often the premises, e.g., buildings to which the subject was referring, while the General Post Office was the company. To differentiate from foreign administrations the term British Post Office (BPO) was also used.

Later chapters will show vehicle liveries across the organisation as better, co-ordinated branding was developed.

One General Post Office?

Correspondence from the Sub-Committee Ninth Meeting 8th of November 1933 Appendix. "Post Office" and "General Post Office."

> "It is clear that the legal and proper title of the Department is
> ***Post Office*** and ***not General Post Office***."

Cromwell's Act of 1657 enacted that 'There be one general office to be called and known by the name of the Post Office of England,' and references in other acts mention the *Post Office* or the 'General Letter (or Post) Office or other Post Office' indicating that the 'General' is not inclusive.

[A section] of the Act of 1908 'revenues arising by or in the General Post Office' was agreed in 1918 to be a drafting error, the more correct term being 'Post Office.'

Almost conclusively, the name **General Post Office** should never have been used as the name of the organisation! Even then, the use of the term General Post Office continued because that is what it had always been called.

Postmaster-General

In other paperwork the crest of the Postmaster-General was used (this later example 1962):

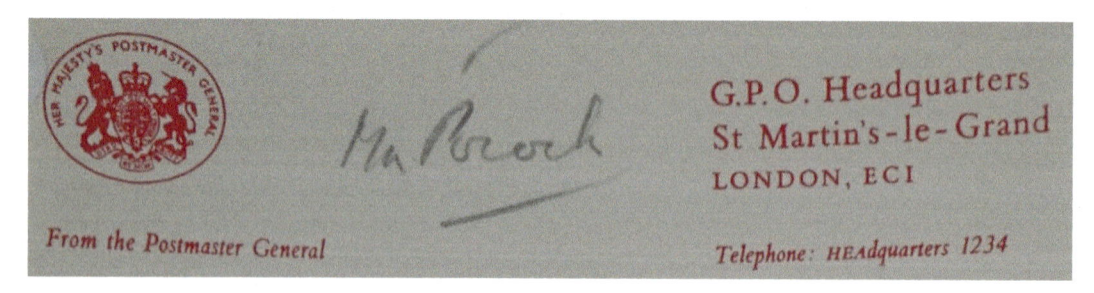

Her Majesty's Postmaster General

The Post Office: 1930s Style

Post offices tended to be functional and smart, but were eminently sober, austere-looking places of business.

Signwriting on post office fascia boards took a cue from Trajan text. Trajan is based on the inscriptional capitals from the Trajan column in Rome, built in 113 AD. *[See earlier chapter Fonts and Foibles.]*

There was a certain amount of standardisation in that every post office had a posting slot (for letters and small parcels), a stamp vending machine, and a clock by which to time the next postal collection.

The post office was literally an office where mail was posted. Additionally, the *Post Office Savings Bank* operated as a function within.

The counters business was the public face of the Post Office.

Top: Finchley post office 1932, POST 118/17181. Above: Post office at 122 Queen Victoria Street, London, on the corner of Old Change Hill in 1938, POST 118/17924. Photos © Royal Mail Group Ltd 2022, courtesy of The Postal Museum.

Styling the Post Office

Combined GPO Premises

Right: Norbury telephone exchange 2013 © J. Osley (Geograph). The post office no longer trades, but a public telephone is retained.

As part of the government, crown estate, it was normal that post offices and telephone exchanges shared premises when it was advantageous to do so. In the example shown, the post office occupied part of the ground floor. A hanging sign (on the far right) confirms that the building is a telephone exchange. The sign above the front door reads 'POST OFFICE - Public Telephone.'

Above: Norbury telephone exchange and post office 1930. Architect: Archibald Scott of the Office of Works. Photo © Royal Mail Group Ltd 2022, courtesy of The Postal Museum. Ref: POST 118/18601.

Styling the POST OFFICE

The Royal Cypher
Historically, the Royal Cypher was, and still is, associated with Royal Mail, carrying the emblem of the reigning monarch, most noticeably on pillar boxes and postal vehicles. The buildings of the Post Office, as a government department, included the Royal Cypher together with the build date, in the same manner that other Crown premises were marked. These cyphers are prolific due partly to the number of new telephone exchanges, and postal sorting offices that were built in the early reign (late 1950s) of Queen Elizabeth II.

POST OFFICE   G R   TELEPHONES.

Southgate Delivery Office
© J. Osley (Geograph)

Erith Telephone Exch.
© Simon Cowper-Smith

Felixstowe Telephone Exch.
© Simon Cowper Smith

Logically it was inevitable that the 'crown device' would appear on products 'supplied for the public service(s).' The Post Office incorporated these 'devices' into its early branding before the GPO monogram was conceived.

"Previously the Post Office has retained its pre-vesting day [October 1969] privilege of using the Crown and Royal Cypher for display on Telecommunications Buildings. It has now been decided by the Design Advisory Committee that the Royal Cypher shall no longer be used on new buildings; there are no plans at present to replace the Cypher by any other symbol." [The ruling also applied to postal buildings.]

THQ memo to Telecommunications Regional Planning Departments 15 June 1971.

Styling the Post Office

King Charles III
Queen Elizabeth II died on 8 September 2022 ending the Elizabethan era. The EIIR cypher signified Elizabeth II Regina. In Latin, queen is Regina, and king is Rex. Charles will use the cypher CIIIR, meaning Charles III Rex, during his reign which will be described as the *Carolean* era.

Use of the GPO name wasn't consistent. This letterhead from the District Manager of Warrington (1912) simply uses POST OFFICE TELEPHONES.

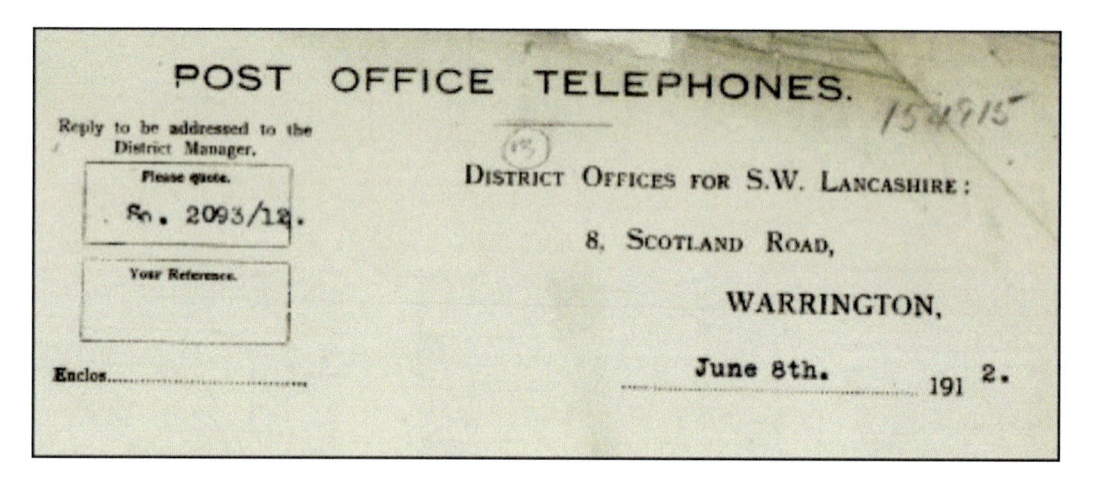

HMSO

His/Her Majesty's Stationery Office (HMSO) supplied printed reports to government departments. It also stocked S.O. (Stationery Office) notebooks which were 'Supplied for the Public Service' and became almost synonymous with the operations of Post Office clerical work.

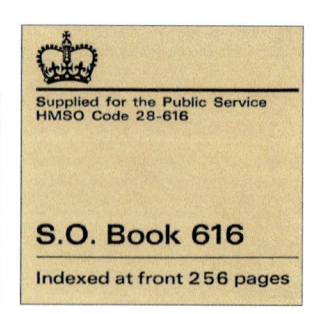

Supplied for the Public Service
HMSO Code 28-616

S.O. Book 616

Indexed at front 256 pages

Sir Stephen Tallents
The appointment of Sir Stephen Tallents as the first Public Relations Officer (PRO) in 1933 led to the GPO taking notice of the need to market its services and be aware of its brand image, within the confines of its public role and accountability to Parliament. Tallents solicited key designers of the era to produce artwork and logos that would produce a coordinated brand.

Styling the POST OFFICE

GPO Monogram 1934-1953

Thus, the first GPO monogram was drawn by graphic designer MacDonald Gill, for a fee of £20.00. The design, which featured the Tudor crown and the letters GPO, was used during the reign of George VI. The typeface, Gill Sans, was created by MacDonald's brother Eric.

"**Gill Sans** *is a humanist sans-serif typeface designed by Eric Gill and released by the British branch of Monotype from* **1928** *onwards.*"

The Tudor Crown, also known as the King's Crown or Imperial Crown, is a widely used symbol in heraldry of the United Kingdom. Officially it was used from 1902 to 1953 representing not only the British monarch personally, but also 'the Crown,' meaning the sovereign source of governmental authority. [From Wiki.]

The first authorised monogram had two concentric circles.

Left: GPO Exhibition in Nottingham 29 May 1934, courtesy of BT Group Archives. Ref: TCB 417/E 8947.

The new monogram was soon updated to a single circle and was then used extensively on publicity and advertising material.

And in 1944 the Council of Industrial Design (CoID) was established with the aim *'to promote by all practicable means the improvement of design in the products of British industry.'*

Styling the Post Office

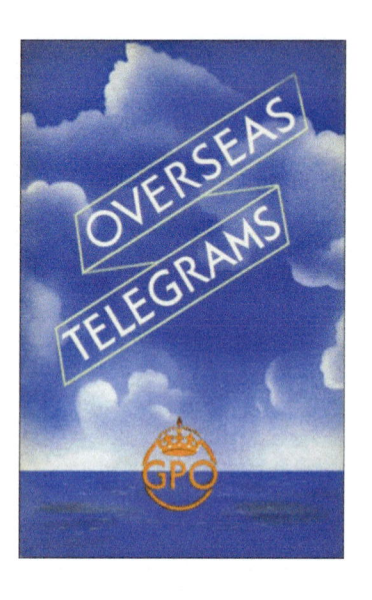

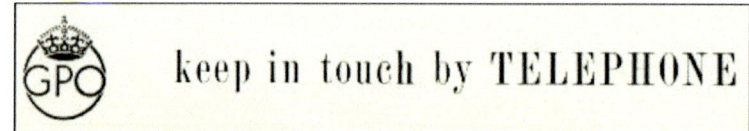

External designers were to heavily influence the progression of the GPO's image. In particular, the Design Research Unit (DRU) founded in 1942 by Herbert Read, Misha Black and Milner Gray, was the first consultancy to combine expertise in architecture, graphics, and industrial design.

GPO Monogram (1953-1969)
The coronation of Queen Elizabeth II, in 1953 prompted a new GPO monogram for which Stuart Rose, an associate of the DRU, was contracted to produce.

The St. Edward's Crown is the centrepiece of the Crown Jewels of the United Kingdom. Named after Saint Edward the Confessor, it has been traditionally used to crown English and British monarchs at their coronations since the 13th century. [From Wiki.]

Thomas Stuart Rose (1911 - 1993)
From 1960-62 Rose was a member of the Stamp Design Committee, and the Post Office Stamp Advisory Panel 1968-76. As a freelancer, he was very influential in design matters for the Post Office such that he succeeded Sir Francis Meynell as Typographical Adviser to the Postmaster-General (Reginald Bevins) in 1962. His appointment as the Post Office's first Design Director, to the postal and Giro businesses, in December 1968, assured his role in continuing to shape the corporate image through the transition of corporation status.

Styling the POST OFFICE

Designed by Stuart Rose, F.S.I.A. who also made the drawing for the covers. Printed by C. Nicholls & Company Ltd., Manchester under contract to H.M. Stationery Office for the Public Relations Department of the General Post Office.

GPO booklet: *The Post Office and you* from mid-1960.

Written by T.E. Johnson in collaboration with the Public Relations Department of the General Post Office.

Scan of booklet from author's collection.

Anthony Wedgwood Benn (1925-2014)
Tony Benn was Postmaster-General between 1964 and 1966 and during his tenure he did much to influence organisational and design polices of the Post Office.

Styling the Post Office

Stuart Rose:

"When he first arrived, Wedgwood Benn had made it known that he intended to promote a new image of the Post Office through its stamps"

[Extract from book *'Royal Mail Stamps -a survey of British stamp design'* 1980 by Stuart Rose.]

David Gentleman (1930 -)

As an artist and RDI (Royal Designer for Industry) David Gentleman's association with the Post Office began in 1962 with an invitation, from the Postmaster-General Tony Benn, to design stamps for National Productivity Year (1962-3). Gentleman went on to successfully draw over 100 different stamps for the Post Office.

Controversially, he suggested that stamp designs would look better if they featured more interesting subjects, but no Queen's head. A compromise was reached which allowed a silhouette profile of the Queen's head and this first appeared on the *Battle of Hastings* stamp set issued in 1966.

Scan of First Day Cover 14 October 1966 from author's collection.

Styling the POST OFFICE

Use of the 1953 GPO Monogram

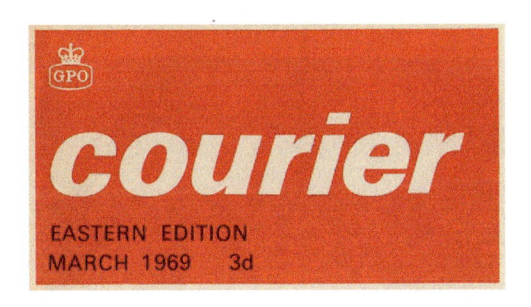

Courier was the staff newspaper which took over from the Post Office Magazine in October 1966.

The price 3d was before the UK adopted decimal currency on 15 February 1971.

In 1969 the re-opened National Postal Museum had capacity to display up to 250,000 stamps in the *King Edward Building*.

Leaflets and scans from author's collection: DLE 570 Telephone Apparatus December 1965; The National Postal Museum; Modern Telephones leaflet PH 1510 (10/1968) designed by C. Vernon & Sons. Ltd.; Mechanising the Mails PL (B) 3000 (7.69).

Styling the Post Office

Telephone: **CEN**tral 1170

GPO HQ letterhead before All-Figure Numbers (AFNs) began to supersede mixed letters and numbers from 1966.

O.H.M.S.

As a government department the Post Office was entitled to use *On Her Majesty's Service (OHMS)* markings when sending correspondence. All postage was settled between the Post Office and HM Treasury.

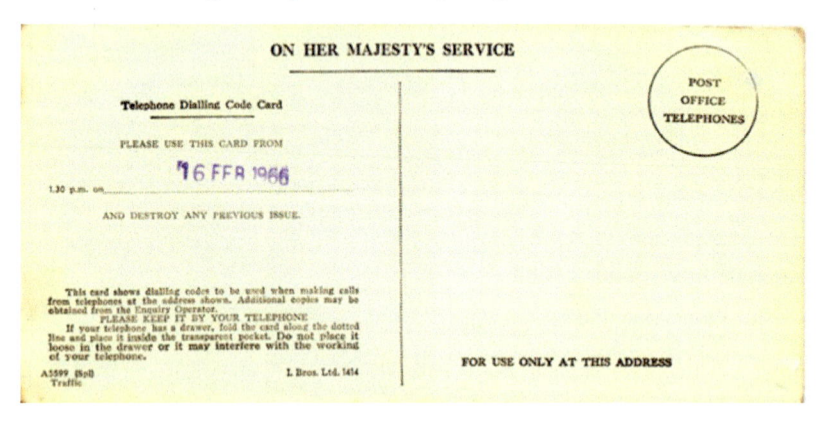

Opposite: A Telephone Dialling Code Card (A5599) dated 1966 from author's collection.

The stiff card allowed them to be sent as postcards direct to subscribers.

[Hansard Volume 784: debated on Tuesday 10 June 1969: '…*all public Departments contribute in full to the Post Office for the costs incurred through the use of prepaid O.H.M.S. postage labels.*]

Opposite: With corporation status in 1969, the OHMS markings were no longer valid, for Post Office use, hence the change to *Official Paid* envelopes.

This example from 1979 is additionally endorsed *P.O. Telecommunications H.Q.*

5.1: Brighter Post Offices

In the organisation that was once known as the General Post Office (GPO), red was well-established as the colour of telephone kiosks, pillar boxes, and Royal Mail vans. Post Offices, the premises of the counter's business, used a simple black typeface without any particular evidence of a brand connected with either Royal Mail or PO Telephones.

The following chapters examine London's showcase offices in the *Brighter Post Offices* project which from the early 1960s eventually evolved into a new style for the business.

Photo: A 21st-century post office prior to opening in a branch of WHS © J. Chenery (2017).

Back to the Sixties

The shop at 555 London Road was a dark and dingy post office [July 1924 to 10/09/1986]. During my early visits (in the 1960s) I couldn't easily see the countertop (I was too short); I could only hear the thumping of the date stamp between the inked pad and my Post Office Savings Bank book.

Below: A Post Office direction (POD) sign (1000-type) atop a pillar box in Debden postal museum store © J. Chenery (2012).

Left: photo courtesy of Nick Skinner [southendtimeline.co.uk] Outside, the pillar box had a direction sign atop pointing towards the post office, and two K6 telephone kiosks, with another sign 'Public Telephone.'

The shop front shows: **F. G. N. Wilson**. A large sign above reads: **Postal and Telegraph Office**. Memory suggests that the counter inside had a wire cage to the ceiling. It was a secure area.

The red pillar box, stamp machine, and associated telephone kiosks all formed a lasting impression on me, a child of the sixties. Elsewhere, (mid-bronze) green *Post Office Telephones* vans tended to faults, at green roadside cabinets, and adjacent footway joint boxes.

Brighter Post Offices

In later years, I'm fairly sure that the counter enclosure was less claustrophobic, but what had prompted this change? **Brighter Post Offices** were first mentioned way back in 1933, and the concept was to be a recurring theme of the Post Office's aim for 'continuous improvement.'

All-Figure Numbers (AFNs)
In what was to be later known as Post Office Telecommunications, the mixed national dialling scheme of letters and numbers was from 1966 onwards to be phased out in favour of All-Figure Numbers, to allow a greater range of numbers and dialling codes to be available.

This eye-catching poster was part of the advertising campaign to encourage telephone users in the 6 *Director Areas* to use the new *All-figure Numbers* before the end of dual working.

The phone service is moving forward

ANN says: dial All-figure Numbers Now.

'ANN will help to add humanity and warmth to what might otherwise have been seen as a somewhat impersonal appeal by the Post Office. The personality of ANN has been created to stimulate public interest and cooperation.'

The K6 Telephone Kiosk
Outside the post office (described) the telephone kiosks had been designed by Sir Giles Gilbert Scott. The K6 *Jubilee kiosk* was commissioned to mark the Silver Jubilee of King George V and Queen Mary in 1935.

Two schemes had helped the proliferation of K6 telephone kiosks:

1. The *Tercentenary Concession* celebrating the Post Office's 300th anniversary (1635 to 1935).
2. The *Jubilee Concession* scheme of 1935 for which the Post Office undertook to provide a kiosk in every village with a post office.

Styling the Post Office

The K6 kiosk of 1936 (manufacture) became a normal sight at many post offices.

Right: K6 telephone kiosks at Hunter Square, Edinburgh © Malcolm Jones (2009).

Below: Edward VII pillar box with stamp machine (5p coin slots) at Notting Hill, London © Dave Bullock (2009).

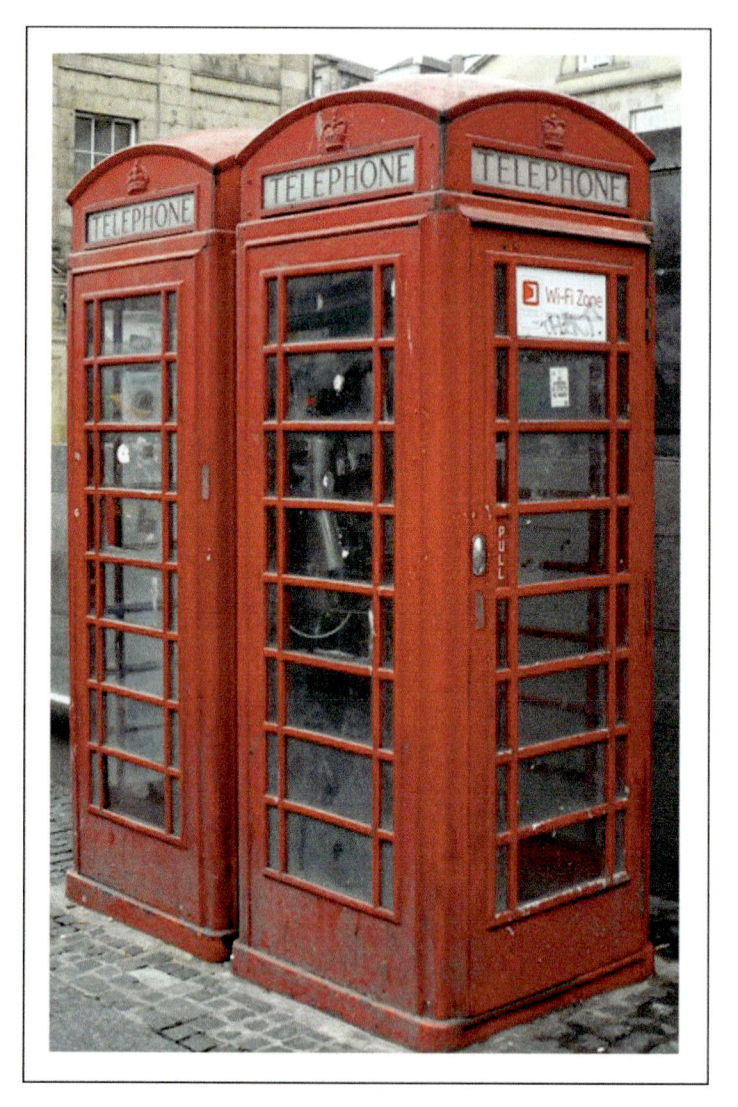

In the 1960s the sale of stamps was limited to post offices and vending machines attached to pillar boxes. The sale of stamps through 'non-post office outlets' (supermarkets and other shops) wasn't considered until 1986.

Brighter Post Offices

The K7 Telephone Kiosk
By the mid-1950s a modern kiosk for *New Towns* was required. [Wiki: *The New Towns Act of 1946 allowed the government to designate areas as new towns.*] The design would also have to incorporate a new coinbox mechanism to work with the soon-to-be-introduced Subscriber Trunk Dialling (STD) system. In 1957 three designers were selected to submit their entries for the new kiosk design. Initial consultations took place with the Council of Industrial Design (CoID) and the Royal Fine Art Commission. The designers chosen were Neville Conder of Sir Hugh Casson & Neville Conder Associates, Misha Black of the DRU, and Jack Howe (Chartered Architect and Industrial Designer). The establishment was generally slow to adopt new ideas and thus the K7 specification stated:

'The finished product will be readily recognisable as a public telephone call office. To assist in this direction some use of the colour **Post Office Red** *will be required in the design and any painted surfaces will be limited to this colour.'*

A 1958 illustration of the proposed K7, courtesy of BT Group Archives. Ref: BTA.0933

On 14 July 1958, the Royal Fine Art Commission noted: *"Mr Conder's design was the best of the three on account of its lightness and elegance."* The final sign-off was by the Post Office Advisory Committee (POAC) before the recommendation was put to the Postmaster-General.

Styling the Post Office

Conder's design was prototyped, and five kiosks were installed, but ultimately the K7's aluminium structure was considered impractical both for ease of fitting the payphone mechanism and public notices, as well as having an unacceptable appearance after prolonged weathering in the British climate.

After considering adapting the design into cast iron, the decision was finally made in February 1965 that '*the Conder design should be abandoned.*'

J. Hodgson for the Post Office department ITD/SSB 31 March 1965: "*…a modern kiosk based on a new design should be produced as quickly as possible.*" [This was to be the K8 model.]

Brighter Post Offices
Meanwhile in the *Post Office Magazine* of July 1959 the Postmaster-General (Ernest Marples) announced plans for 'Brighter Post Offices,' and new 'economy' designs for all Post Office buildings, with a Head Post Office for Hitchin and a Telephone Exchange at Altrincham.

A Joint Post Office/Ministry of Works, Research and Development Group had been formed in 1957 to find ways of getting better value for money spent on post office buildings, consistent with efficiency and good neighbourliness. It was envisaged that reduced costs and universal designs would satisfy the accountants and the public.

As a result of the Post Office Act 1961, the Post Office enjoyed a degree of financial autonomy comparable with the nationalised industries.

Specifically, the Postmaster-General engaged well-known designers:

- Sir Hugh Casson and Professor Misha Black, (recognised for the South Bank Festival of Britain). Black was co-founder of the Design Research Unit (DRU)

- Mr W L Stevenson, Principal of the Liverpool College of Art

- Ormrod and Partners, including architect Derek Jones

Brighter Post Offices

With a brief to modernise six 'old-fashioned' Branch Offices (BOs) in four cities:

- Three BOs in London
- Leeds: Chapeltown Road
- Liverpool: Corn Exchange
- Manchester: Royal Exchange

As reported: *"The designers produced some novel ideas. They came up with new designs for glass counter screens. They suggested new materials: vitreous enamel counter fronts, blockboard panelling for walls, and extensive use of satin-finished aluminium. They suggested imaginative colour schemes: red, blue, green, and white at the Royal Exchange, white, grey, black and scarlet in the London offices. All the designs were light, airy and exciting. We can get away from the old atmosphere of heavy mahogany counters, dark bronze grilles, dull cream walls and cumbersome business notices."*

Chapeltown Rd., BO, Leeds was completed and reopened in October 1960, and followed by Liverpool BO on 5 December.

The *Post Office Magazine* of January 1961 reported: *"Visitors noticed a bright new red standing out in the colour scheme.* The men who chose it, W.L. Stevenson, the industrial designer, and D.H. Jones the architect told why they used it instead of our traditional Post Office Red. Mr Stevenson said he wanted to use a lively and recognisable heraldic colour in place of the old red and black scheme.

"The old Post Office Red, used with black and other colours, is dead," said Mr Jones. *"We have used the orange-red with black or white or stainless steel. These bring the red out; they 'send it,' to use the modern idiom."*

This appears to be the first use of a new shade of red in the Post Office. The decor wasn't uniformly applied across the chosen sites, but the project prompted the Post Office to seek a universally standard design.

The *Post Office Report and Accounts* (1962/3) quoted *"The public part of new post office buildings will be assembled from a set of standardised, and to a large extent, prefabricated components. The dominant feature of the exterior will be a prominent red illuminated transom-bar bearing the words POST OFFICE."*

This transom-bar was finished in what was to become known as *House-style* red, a brighter shade than *Post Office Red*.

Styling the Post Office

Later, the Post Office Magazine of August 1963 reported: *The joint group has produced standard designs for the Altrincham type telephone exchange and is working on plans for standardising the larger K-type exchange.*

The trundling bureaucracy of the Post Office meant that these plans took a long time to be fully implemented, such was the size of the GPO estate. Re-organisation (1969) and UK metrication (1971) compounded the task.

In London, the trial 'Brighter post offices' at:
- South Molton Street

- Knightsbridge

- New Bridge Street/corner of Tudor Street (aka Ludgate Circus)

…were all successfully modernised between 1960 and 1962 {See chapters 5.3, 5.4, 5.5}.

While further trials and refurbishments of *Brighter Post Offices* were ongoing, the demand for new post office premises was met by best practice and increased self-service facilities, such as the provision of inset vending machines for stamps, envelopes and stationery.

A new 'flagship' branch office, with service 24-hours a day was opened near to Trafalgar Square, in November 1962. Although this post office included self-service elements of the era, it still warranted a 33-position staffed counter to cope with the volume of customers, letters, packets and parcels. {See chapter 5.6}.

The next chapter introduces the first two Post Office premises that were built for economy, and pre-dated the culmination of what was to become *House Style* {chapter 5.7} for post offices.

5.2: Building with Economy

Altrincham Telephone Exchange (1960)
The 1960s were to be a technologically important decade for the Post Office as new designs of buildings, telephone equipment, stamp vending machines, post offices, and microwave towers were all under development.

Altrincham (Cheshire) was a new 10,000 line Director (Strowger) exchange in Manchester Area. It was built as a single storey on a large vacant site adjacent to the existing NTC (1908) exchange. A stark contrast in design.

Above: Altrincham Telephone Exchange 1963, courtesy of BT Group Archives. Ref: TCB 473/P 8816.
Top right: The old NTC exchange 1908 © Mark Skillen (April 2022).

Styling the Post Office

Altrincham TE (1960)
PO Report and Accounts 1960/1: *'Completed on 5 July 1960... Altrincham points the way to economies in exchange building in the future.'*

POTJ Autumn 1959: *'Among other features the apparatus room will have continuous windows at high level which give lighting throughout without the need for roof lighting. Cables enter just above ground level, thus eliminating the need for the usual basement cable chamber and are carried on bearers along the inner face of the apparatus room external wall. Cables will be encased above floor level, with removable panels. The design will enable extension with minimum disturbance to switching-equipment.*

Left: Altrincham Telephone Exchange under repair © Mark Skillen (April 2022).

Above: Altrincham Telephone Exchange 1963, courtesy of BT Group Archives. Ref: TCB 473/P 8815.

Building with Economy

In these early years of the 1960s the Post Office formed partnerships between the government's Ministry of Works and its architects, research development groups, numerous departments within the Post Office as well as specialist external engineers and contractors. Often the lengthy bureaucracy involved in decision-making, and trials over many years conspired to negate longer-term cost savings. However, some schemes were encouragingly successful.

Leighton Buzzard TE (1963)

'*A NEW type of telephone exchange building housing more than 2,000 lines is springing up throughout the country. It is the single storey K-type building which because it is designed to standardised plans, is quicker and cheaper to plan and is playing a valuable role in meeting the increasing need for more exchanges. Twenty-two others are at present in course of construction and forty more will be completed within the next few years.*' [POTJ Autumn 1964.]

Above: Leighton Buzzard TE 1933, courtesy of BT Group Archives. Ref: TCB 417/E 28319.

Planned in 1961, Leighton Buzzard was the first K-type exchange building, completed in February 1963. It was also notable in being the home of the experimental TXE1 electronic exchange which was BIS 23 May 1968 relieving a UAX7 and Linslade MNDX. However, the through-traffic in the area required a larger building which was subsequently constructed in 1972 and equipped with two TXE2s and exceptionally a TXE6. These were later replaced with a TXE4 serving 10,000 lines.

Styling the Post Office

Hitchin Head Post Office (1962). Architect: John Stevens

A modern post office for the 1960s. Note the large overhanging fascia board which boldly proclaims POST OFFICE & SAVINGS BANK. Until c2011, National Savings & Investments attracted much of its business from the post offices; dual branding was most valuable.

The Joint Post Office/Ministry of Works and Research Development Group (RDG) contracted a new Head Post Office at a cost of only £64,000 instead of the expected price of £100,000.

Right: Hitchin Head Post Office © Jelm6 on Flickr (August 2009) with CC licence. The office closed in 2012. Demolition took place in 2014 for redevelopment of the site.

Above: Hitchin Head Post Office, 90 Hermitage Road opened 12 February 1962. Photo © Royal Mail Group Ltd 2022, courtesy of The Postal Museum. Ref: POST 120/2500.

Building with Economy

Some of these economy buildings may not have been entirely suitable for repurposing in later decades, but ultimately Hitchin HPO and sorting office had its fate sealed by the 'economies of scale' whereby fewer, bigger sorting offices could handle greater volumes of mail, in a declining letters' market. Online postage, electronic money transfers, together with executive agencies choosing not to trade via Post Office Counters, all hastened its demise. The split of POC from Royal Mail, and the government no longer wishing to subsidise loss-making parts of the businesses changed the long-established post office network forever. In the 1960s it may have been envisaged that self-service machines would have played more of a part in the run-down of staffed post offices…

Self-Service Machines
Stamp Vending Machines (SVMs) and self-service featured strongly in the design of new post office shopfronts. Until circa 1986, books of postage stamps could only be purchased from post office premises or SVMs, thus these self-service units were far more commonplace than in later decades.

Self-service panel for post offices, styled by Douglas Scott Associates and manufactured by Associated Automation and GPO Engineering Department.

Heading strip: Stamped Stationery, Postage Stamps.

Vertical oblongs are various SVM (Stamp Vending Machine) denominations.

Top horizontal slots are 'letter card' and 'envelope.'

Above: Hitchin HPO, self-service panel 1962. Photo © Royal Mail Group Ltd 2022, courtesy of The Post Museum. Ref: POST 118/17755.

Styling the Post Office

Self-Service Machines

The GPO Engineering Department collaborated with Douglas Scott Associates and Associated Automation to produce various self-service machines, both free standing and inset into walls, as well as custom panels on post office shop fronts.

A self-service machine inset to the wall of the DO (Delivery Office) at Chesterfield © John Murdoch (2022). A time-warp of the long-gone GPO monogram, and mosaic tiles from the 1960s. The posting box element remained in use until July 2006.

Chesterfield DO is on a site adjacent to *Future Walk*, a Post Office HQ which currently stands in place of the former AGD (Accountant Generals Department), once well-known for administering Post Office pensions. The AGD was opened by the PMG on 28 November 1963 as the department relocated 1600 staff from London as part of the government's policy (post-WWII) of dispersing work out of the Capital. The AGD building known as Chetwynd House was finally demolished in 1997.

5.3: South Molton Post Office

South Molton Street Post Office at 65 South Molton Street, City of Westminster.

Of the trial *Brighter Post Offices*, Gordon Pocock (Sites & Buildings branch of HQ) wrote in the Post Office Magazine of August 1960:

" These six offices will all be finished soon. South Molton Street Branch Office has been finished already - at the end of July (1960)."

Above: South Molton Branch Office 1963. Photo © Royal Mail Group Ltd 2022, courtesy of The Postal Museum. Ref: POST 118/17689.

Styling the Post Office

Old and New

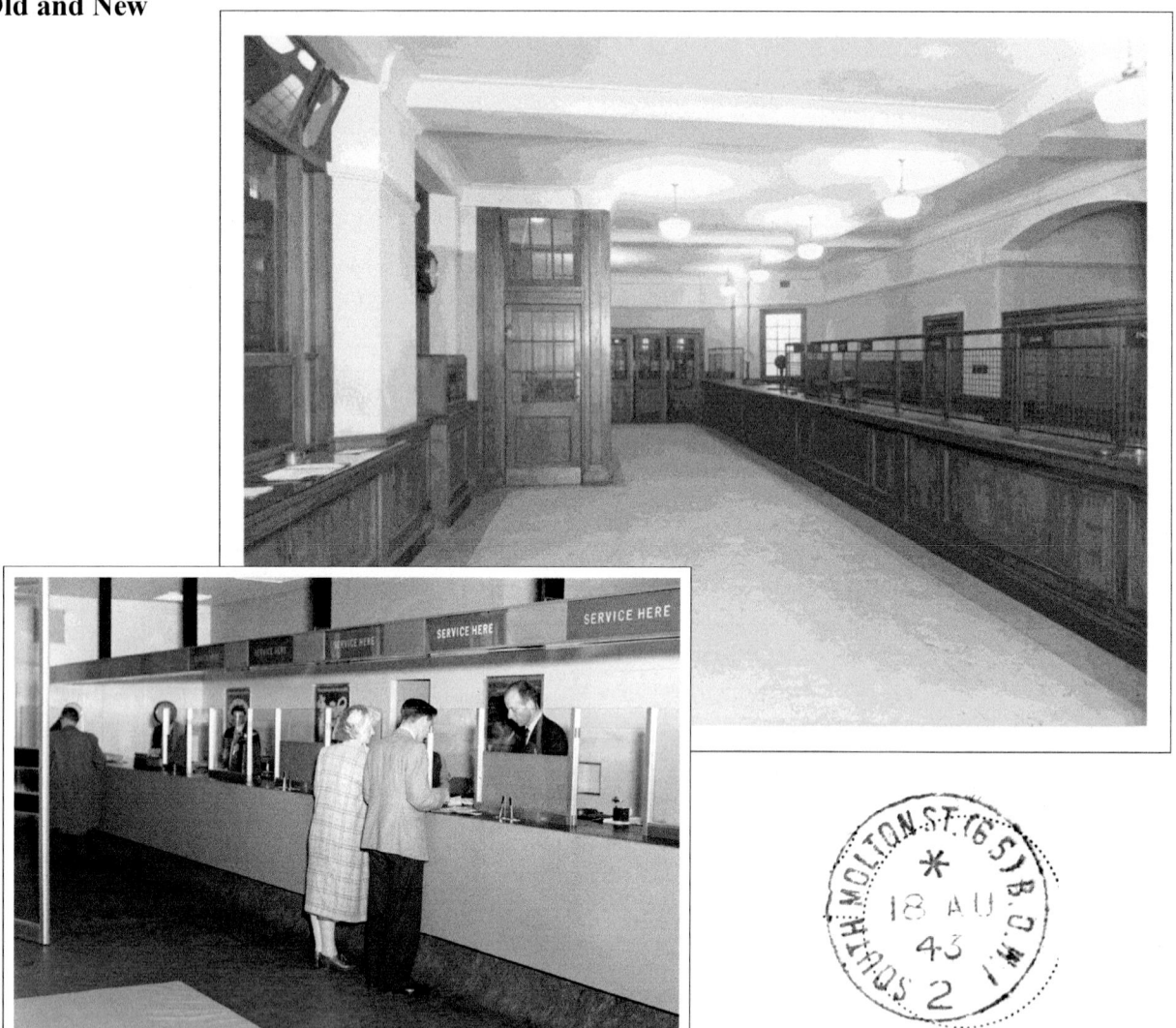

Top: South Molton Street 1931. Ref: POST 118/18686. Left: South Molton Street 1960. Ref: POST 118/ 18111. The dull metal counter grill has been replaced by modern glass giving a more open feel to the office.
Photos © Royal Mail Group Ltd 2022, courtesy of The Postal Museum.

A Modern Look

*Above: South Molton Street 1960. Ref: POST 118/17839.
Photo © Royal Mail Group Ltd 2022, courtesy of The Postal Museum.*

Post Office Magazine September 1960:

"The New Look—a modern bright office; the main colours are black, white and grey, but with patches of green and bright red on the counter notices and screen. Note the new flush ceiling with recessed lights and the experimental glass screen with no louvres."

Styling the Post Office

South Molton Exterior
Photo © Royal Mail Group Ltd 2022, courtesy of The Postal Museum.

Left: 1960, the 'new' experimental Post Office sign (Clarendon type) with crown symbol. Ref: POST 118/18299.

Later sites in the trials had a new standardised hanging sign.

Above: In 1960 the SAVINGS BANK was still part of the Post Office and thus is featured in one of the red transom bars across the windows.

Right: A red telephone kiosk nearby harkens back to a forgotten age long-before cellular phones.

Right: A red K6 kiosk, in the middle of the pedestrianised street, retains a Post Office connection © Nigel Turner (2020). The nearby South Molton Street BO (closed 26/01/1996) is now a Thomas Sabo jeweller's shop.

5.4: Knightsbridge Post Office

At 55 Knightsbridge, Belgravia, SW1 [1961 re-opening]

Above: Knightsbridge BO 1961. Ref: POST 118/2466. A wood-fronted counter with glass screen. Photo © Royal Mail Group Ltd 2022, courtesy of The Postal Museum.

Posters behind the counter advise: *Pack your parcels carefully. Use recorded delivery. Please use your correct address.* The counter scales are manufactured by *Avery* and display the GPO monogram.

55 Knightsbridge

Councillor R. L. Everest, Mayor of Westminster, formally opened the modernised Knightsbridge B.O. in July 1961. [Post Office Magazine July 1961.]

Above: Knightsbridge BO 1962. Ref: POST 118/2467.
Photo © Royal Mail Group Ltd 2022, courtesy of The Postal Museum.

Note the square post office sign hanging on the wall (top left), with matching font on the transom bar. The self-service slots facing the street are 'Stamps and change' and 'Stamped Stationery.'

Façade Elements

"At present the nearest approach to the new house style is the Knightsbridge Post Office exterior which has a metal frame front, red transom bar, new clock, self-service machines, and an information panel. Designers Mish Black and Alexander Gibson of DRU and Sir Hugh Casson."

The Façade:

CLOCK
SELF SERVICE SUITE
SIGN
TRANSOM
NOTICES
POSTERS
POSTING BOX
UNIFIED TYPOGRAPHY

Further reading: DESIGN (mag) No.173 May 1963.

Above: Outside the Knightsbridge office, the hanging sign was the one used at trial sites. The graphics designer was Ronald Armstrong of the DRU. The handstamp shown is after the branch reopened at SW7 in 2001, replacing Lancelot Place BO.

A definitive *House Style* was to take many more years to formulate; the sign evoked much discussion. An updated sign was affixed to the modernised Mount Pleasant BO in November 1964. [See chapter 5.7. for photo.]

"When the question of whether to adopt this sign for general use was being considered it was thought that the words 'Post Office' would lose some of their impact by being split up. This feature would be more pronounced if the GPO emblem were used instead of a Crown." [Memo to PMG from K. H. Cadbury December 1964.]

"...the PMG has approved the series of signs for Post Office buildings using the GPO device above the words 'Post Office', 'Telephones', and 'Overseas Telegraph Office' respectively."
[Memo to Stuart Rose from T. A. O'Brien 29 Jan 1965.]

Styling the Post Office

By August 1967, a further revised sign was to be fitted to Lombard Street BO. In February 1969, with a batch of *House Style* signs on order, it was realised that the GPO name would cease to exist after Vesting Day, and that interim arrangements for a new sign would need to be considered.

Banks and Miles double-line alphabet

Above: Knightsbridge BO 1984. Ref: POST 118/PF0461.
Photo © Royal Mail Group Ltd 2022, courtesy of The Postal Museum.

This much later photo depicts the *Banks and Miles* double-line alphabet, yellow font on a red background. An oval Post Office sign has replaced the square *House Style* version. A *National Girobank* plate is affixed to the corner pillar. Knightsbridge BO closed finally on 13 June 1984.

By 2011 Harvie & Hudson shirtmakers occupied the premises. In 2020 the Grade II listed block was being redeveloped, with the 120m long façade, dating back to 1903, retained.

5.5: Ludgate Circus Post Office

The Branch Office at 16-18 New Bridge Street, EC4 was reopened on 21 June 1962 by Mr Cecil H King, chairman of Daily Mirror Newspapers.

Above: Ludgate Circus BO 1962 at the corner of New Bridge Street and Tudor Street. Ref: POST 118/18520. Photo © Royal Mail Group Ltd 2022, courtesy of The Postal Museum.

Ludgate Circus was one of the biggest and busiest post offices in the City of London, which is why it was chosen as one of the trial sites for the *Brighter Post Offices* project. Note the square-shaped 'POST OFFICE' hanging sign(s) years before the more familiar oval-shaped signs were devised.

Styling the Post Office

Gordon Pocock (Sites & Buildings branch of HQ) wrote in POM August 1960:

"Our plans are not just for a new look for six special post offices, but for all our old-fashioned offices. They are part of the New Look for the Post Office."

Left: Ludgate Circus counter 1933. Ref: POST 118/5136. "The old counter with its heavy mahogany front, bronze grille and dangling notices has been swept away and replaced with a new counter faced in waxed teak, with a light glass screen and an elegant line of illuminated notices above."

Above: This was a typical style counter in post offices prior to the 1960s. Solid wood counter with secure grills.

Right: Ludgate Circus counter 1962. Ref: POST 118/17798.

Photos © Royal Mail Group Ltd 2022, courtesy of The Postal Museum.

Ludgate Circus Post Office

The New Look

Big and spacious, the high ceiling was dictated by the architecture of the building.

Modernisations of branch offices that were once in the style of *Post Office Georgian* couldn't fully escape the past image.

Above: Ludgate Circus counter 1962. Ref: POST 118/18515.

Right: Ludgate Circus counter 1962. Ref: POST 118/17802.

Photos © Royal Mail Group Ltd 2022, courtesy of The Postal Museum.

Post & Go

Ludgate Circus was an early adopter of Post & Go, having the first unit installed 15 October 2008 in the BO. Ultimately there were four P & G units, and two stamp vending machines (SVMs) in the P & G suite, in its heyday. See chapter 15, *Post Office Counters* for more.

Above: Post & Go sign © Sludge G from Flickr with CC licence (2009).
Left: The former premises at New Bridge Street © Dave Collier (2010).

Ludgate Circus BO closed on 22 April 2009. In Tudor Street, a section of the premises was partitioned-off to become 18A New Bridge Street, and a dedicated *Post & Go* self-service suite was opened on 21 April 2009. The *Post & Go* office finally closed during 2015.

5.6: Trafalgar Square Post Office

"One of the finest Post Offices in Europe" at 24-28 William IV Street, London WC2.

Trafalgar Square Branch Office (BO) © *Malcolm Jones (2013).*

Trafalgar Square post office was located on the corner of Adelaide Street and William IV Street, London, WC2. It opened on 27 November 1962. The postal architect was Philip Watkinson of the Public Building & Works. The new office replaced three other branches around Trafalgar Square that were coming to the end of their leases. This included Charing Cross BO which originally opened circa 1845.

Mike Horne: *"It was one of the first new post offices to demonstrate the new corporate identity, adopted by the GPO (General Post Office) for its customer-facing premises."*

Post Office Magazine:
September 1962: *The intention is to have all 1800 main post offices smartened up by about 1968 at a cost of £300,000 a year.*

January 1963: *EVERYBODY will instantly recognise the local post office when he sees it. That is one aim of the new house-style for post-offices, announced recently by the PMG. Another aim is to present a bright, modern face.*

Styling the Post Office

Progress

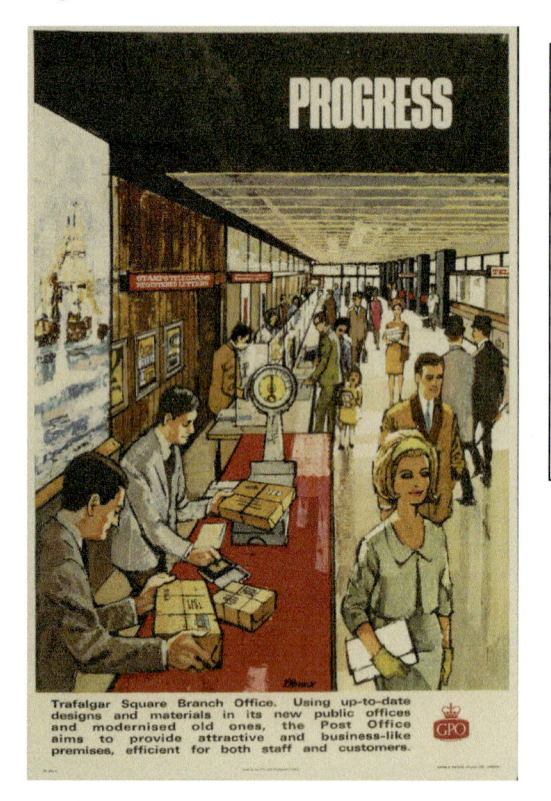

Trafalgar Square Branch Office. Using up-to-date designs and materials in its new public offices and modernised old ones, the Post Office aims to provide attractive and business-like premises, efficient for both staff and customers.

Left: Internal poster (c1966) issued by the Joint Production Council (JPC) on the subject of modernisation. Artist: Hanna, R. Printed by Moore & Matthes Ltd. Ref: POST 110/1673.

Right: The parcels counter 1962. Ref: POST 118/17628.

PARCELS
STAMPS
TELEGRAMS
REGISTERED LETTERS

Photo/poster © Royal Mail Group Ltd 2022, courtesy of The Postal Museum.

Trafalgar Square Post Office

Such was the demand for counter services this new branch was reportedly open 24-hours a day.

There were 26 self-service machines for stamps and envelopes. Inside, the very long counter had 33 serving positions.

Postbox № WC2 83, William IV Street.

Above: This postbox is actually three boxes of a nonstandard design, set into the wall © 2014 Chris Downer {Geograph.org.uk/p/3847815}

Trafalgar Square BO was featured in the Post Office Magazine of January 1963. The frontage of the post office once ran the entire length of William IV Street with entrances/exits on each corner, Adelaide Street and St. Martin's Place.

Right: A busy exterior scene showing the many stamp machines in use 1962. Ref: POST 118/17940. Photo © Royal Mail Group Ltd 2022, courtesy of The Postal Museum.

Trafalgar Square BO: Public Telephones Lower Ground Floor

STD, Subscriber Trunk Dialling for the City of London Area was possible from about mid-1961 thus, the *new* pay-on-answer coinboxes were fitted here.

Left: Making a call on the new coinbox telephone. Year: 1962. Ref: TCB 473/P 8252.

'Sound-insulated and doodle-proofed booths.'

[These were presumed to be of a stainless steel lattice.]

Right: Open-tread stairs leading down to the payphone vestibules. Year: 1962. Ref: TCB 473/P 8251.

Photos courtesy of BT Group Archives.

Trafalgar Square Post Office

Posting Slots and Parcel Chutes

STAMP BOOKS save time

Above: The GPO monogram branding features on the scales and posting slots. Ref: POST 118/18610.

Right: Parcels and packets followed chutes which led to the lower ground for sorting. Ref: POST 118/17680. Year: 1962/3

Photos © Royal Mail Group Ltd 2022, courtesy of The Postal Museum.

Trafalgar Square BO closed permanently on 24 December 2018. Commercial challenges and the changing shape of the high street were reasons cited for its closure.

An Overview of House Style(s)

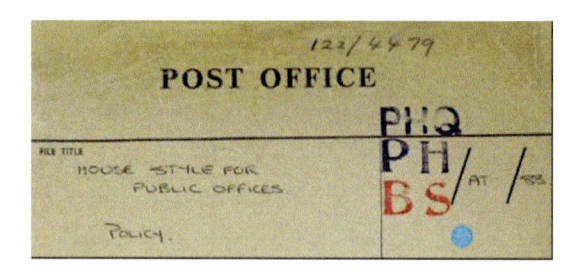

The *Brighter Post Offices* project was optimistic in its approach to a *New Look* for post office branches and the wider GPO image. Aside from the six trial conversion sites, the new Trafalgar Square BO (Nov 1962) incorporated the best elements for a consistently modern design. The provisioning of new post offices couldn't be halted simply because the ultimate style was still being sought.

By July 1962, it had been decided to study the evolution of post office styles and to mount an exhibition to showcase past, present, and future (possible) styles, as well as considerations for custom-made building panels, as identified in the *Building with Economy* project(s) that had been tried at Altrincham and Hitchin. The designs were to feature standardised slot-in building panels to present a coherent image and ultimately lead to cost-savings.

On 1 August 1962, the GPO, together with what had now become the Ministry of Public Buildings and Works (MPB&W), staged an extensive exhibition in the Assembly Hall on the second floor of Fleet Building (home of the Central Telegraph Office), London. *A House Style for Post Offices* set out, for the 'movers and shakers' of the time, a vision for the standardisation, simplicity, uniformity, and style for new and refurbished post offices.

The GPO's corporate identity was neither easy to define, or to change. Use of the royal crown was vested in the Queen, and the public's perception of the connection between Royal Mail, the Post Office, and the GPO was never clear.

Retrospectively, in *Design* (magazine) of May 1963, David Wainwright wrote:

"In the exhibition, the details of accessories were mostly taken from the Hugh Casson/Misha Black schemes. ...The Post Office seems to be a long way from achieving a house style in detail."

As both a DRU associate and contractor to the GPO, Stuart Rose worked on the typography of the Clarendon letterset, which was used in the project. This coincided with Rose replacing Francis Meynell as Typographical Adviser to the PMG (Reginald Bevins) in October 1962.

The GPO's *House Style* was further developed by Eric Bedford [Ministry of Public Buildings & Works architect and designer of PO Tower].

5.7: House Style

A House Style for Post Offices (1 August 1962)

"This display has been mounted to show the development of the design of public post offices and Post Office ideas about the future. After all the work that has been put in over the past few years, we can now evolve a standard style for public post offices which will be in a modern idiom, make use of modern techniques and materials, and make public post offices instantly recognisable as such."

In Fleet Building, an exhibition was staged with a more-than 50-panel showcase detailing the evolution of post offices, past, present, and future.

Left: A House Style for Post Offices, 1962 exhibition, courtesy of BT Group Archives. Ref: TCB 473/P 8189.

Past: The Post Office's house-style in the 1930s was of the old bronze and mahogany design generally contained in a Neo-Georgian building, which included a heavy wooden counter and furniture with a bronze grille and fittings.

"This style was all right in its day, and quite distinctive, but is now old-fashioned."

Styling the Post Office

Present: After the war the Post Office management and staff together undertook a thorough review of its needs. Offices consequently moved into a more modern idiom and are more light and spacious; there is a glass screen; but there is no longer any uniform style.

Future: In the last few years there has been change and experiment. The Post Office has called in design consultants who have modernised six offices, embodying positive ideas for a house-style. We need to assess the results and work them into one consistent style.

Stuart Rose's Clarendon alphabet on display in Fleet Building exhibition in 1962.

The example panels showed the typical public notices/signs that would be used in the counter's business.

Left: House Style lettering, courtesy of BT Group Archives TCB 473/P 8307.

In a letter to the Reginald Bevins, Postmaster-General (PMG) on 7 November 1962, A.H. Ridge promulgated:

"The introduction of the house-style is an important landmark in the development of our services and one which might prove extremely popular. The house-style is intended primarily for new offices, but we shall greatly increase its impact if we can include one or two of its key features (for example, the external sign and transom bar) in modernised offices."

An updated exhibition was staged on 19 November 1962 at which the PMG issued a press release and announced that five post offices would implement the newly formulated and refined *House-Style*. Further dates in November allowed public viewing of the project.

House Style

Five Trial House-Style Sites

Mount Pleasant BO, EC1
Mill Hill BO, NW7
South-West District Office, SW1
Temple Fortune BO, NW11
Brondesbury BO, (Brent) NW6
Ealing BO, W5

As requested below, Stuart Rose revised the design of the external hanging sign that was used at Knightsbridge BO, so that it included the GPO monogram rather than simply the crown.

A memo to F B Savage DPRO from GJ Pocock on 16 Aug 1962: *"The DG has now agreed that we should push ahead with the house-style idea with the maximum possible speed, subject to working out details of cost and design. The standard sign must include the new typography as amended by Stuart Rose. We think the design of the actual crown could be tidied up."*

There was much debate about signage, enough to warrant an explanation:

"In 1954 a sub-committee on PO Savings Facilities recommended that 'Savings Bank' should appear on the external signs for public offices. This was accepted at a DWC meeting in April 1955 and a redesigned sign was introduced. In August 1963, Mr. Stuart Rose's design for the external sign, which does not include 'Savings Bank' was approved by the then PMG and adopted as standard."

Postmaster-General's Newsletter No. 34: November 1962
The dominant feature of the exterior of the new post offices will be a façade of standard prefabricated metal panels, each ten feet high and six feet wide, across which, at the top, will be a prominent red illuminated transom bearing the words: "POST OFFICE" and "SAVINGS BANK". Each office will also have an additional external sign which says "POST OFFICE" only. The metal panels will be adapted to take doors, telephone kiosks, posting boxes, window notices, vending machines, posters and so on. There will be some scope for variation of colour and material in the infill at the base of the panels but nowhere else.

Mount Pleasant BO

1968: Mount Pleasant BO used a new sign which displayed the GPO monogram and reinforced the brand connection that post offices were part of the GPO. Ref: POST 118/15432.
Photo © Royal Mail Group Ltd 2022, courtesy of The Postal Museum.

"In order to keep costs within the prescribed limits the house-style should not be incorporated in modernised offices generally, except for one or two superficial features, such as the external sign."
A.H. Ridge 2 April 1963. [Mount Pleasant BO *House Style* was completed circa April 1964.]

At this stage, the *Brighter Post Offices/House Style* concept was still in the process of being costed, sourced and implemented with all of the usual caution and bureaucracy that typified the GPO.

Abergavenny BO

Abergavenny, 1984. Ref: POST 118/PF0328. This BO is a typical example of the persisting red transom bars of the House-Style design. Although (from 1969) the Post Office no longer governed the Savings Bank, it still operated as an agency for them. Exceptionally, by now, the Giro/Girobank sign is a separate one, and not part of the transom lettering. Photo © Royal Mail Group Ltd 2022, courtesy of The Postal Museum.

Red Transom Bars

Typically, the red transom bars (shown above) featured: **TELEPHONES, POST OFFICE, SAVINGS BANK.**

It was decided that if the frontage of a post office was too narrow to incorporate multiple transom bars, then the **SAVINGS BANK** would be omitted, and only the **POST OFFICE** name would be used. Such was the attention to detail, and the procrastination of the GPO consultative processes.

By Feb 1970, opinion had changed, and the committee endorsed the example which showed the words **POST OFFICE** in capital lettering on alternative units, and on the other units **Giro** (new from 1968), **Savings Bank**, and **Telephones** in smaller lettering.

Further Progress in Design
As can be seen, even minor changes in the GPO organisation took years to be discussed, developed, agreed, modified, and finally implemented. Decision-making was woefully slow as every possible solution was investigated. In June 1970 it was stated: Four forms of transom panel will be available from the Post Office from 1 July 1970. Three will be lettered and one plain; the lettering will be white on a background of Postal Service Red. The four panels are as follows:

POST OFFICE, **Telephones**, **Giro** [at either end] **Savings Bank**, **Unlettered**.

End of House Style
8 May 1978: *"It has been decided that the house-style concept introduced in 1970 for new or modernised public office schemes will no longer be used. An instruction is being sent to Regions informing them of this decision."*

Postscript
This was by no means the end of red transom panels, but back in 1965 the Post Office was about to examine its whole corporate image, as preparations for the change to Corporation status were about to start. This overlapped the *Brighter Post Offices* transformation and brought up numerous additional questions.

The implementation of House-Style and subsequent design changes were a long, drawn-out process over several decades for which thousands of memos were circulated. The narratives shown here are but a fraction of the full correspondence as the Post Office decision-making process trundled on. The shade of red used for the transom panels was the subject of even greater scrutiny, as will be seen in the chapter *'Saga of Postal Services Red.'*

New PMG
In late 1964, Tony Benn MP was appointed the new PMG in Harold Wilson's government. Benn had great aspirations to modernise everything in the GPO and planned three separate businesses, Postal, Telecommunications, and what was (from 1968) to be National Giro (now absorbed into Santander). The long-established National Savings (Post Office Savings Bank) remained with the Exchequer. Realising that each business would require a separate, but co-ordinated identity, the GPO engaged on the recommendation of the CoID, the services of Frederick Henri Kay (FHK) Henrion in January 1965. Henrion had produced posters for the Ministry of Information; his corporate design work was well-established.

6.1: Saga of Postal Services Red

Introduction

As the Post Office made plans to split its businesses (and ultimately achieve corporation status) its quest for the perfect corporate image had already spanned many years. Its *Brighter Post Offices* projects led to a formal *House-Style* (if only for post offices) from about 1964 and produced a red-coloured transom bar, and standardised external hanging-sign. These styles were becoming the immediately recognisable, distinguishing features of the post office counters business, but far more was needed. An external consultant was engaged to assist with the creation of a coordinated style for the whole organisation, but with differentiation of Posts/Telecoms, and Banking. During this period, the iconic red branding was subtly changed to a different shade, much to the surprise of other departments in the company! This chapter delves into the details of how the famous shade of red was changed, almost unwittingly, across the upcoming corporation.

Post Office Red

Since the first painting of pillar boxes in a shade of red, in London from c1874, the colour had continued to be associated with the General Post Office. The ubiquitous *Post Office Red* telephone kiosk has reinforced this brand image of typical Britishness, together with the red Royal Mail vans seen daily on our streets. The GPO's standard design of telephone kiosk, the K1 of the 1920s was specified to have Oxide Red paint for its metal window frames. The woodwork of the door was treated with paint, finishing, *Special Red*. The K3 also used *Special Red*. Kiosks K2 and K4 had *Flame* (red) paint internally, and *Special Red* externally. British Standard paint colours were introduced in 1930 and were adopted mainly by government departments, the service industry, and the military. Thus, the new K6 Jubilee telephone kiosk of 1935 was specified to be finished in *Post Office Red* to BS381 shade no. 38. In 1948 the paint scheme was revised to BS381C, and the shade was renumbered to 538. Another benchmark, the BS2660 range *Colours for Building and Decorative Paints* wasn't introduced until 1955. The K7 of 1962 was specified to include elements of *Post Office Red*, but this kiosk wasn't adopted beyond a limited trial.

House Style Red

The red transom bar of the experimental *Brighter Post Offices* project was finished in what became known as *House-Style* red.

Styling the Post Office

In the *Post Office Magazine* of January 1961 the article *Singing Red comes out with a Bing* introduced a shade of red that was first used in the *Brighter Post Offices* project for Chapeltown Road BO, Leeds in October 1960.

"Compare 'Singing Red' with the old colour; we've used it in this edition [the header] of the Magazine. 'Singing Red' contains more orange than Post Office Red, and really is that old friend vermilion we found in our childhood paint boxes. And it is said to be softer on the eye."

Henri Henrion Design Associates

In early 1965 at the behest of the Postmaster-General, Henrion was invited to investigate the branding of the Post Office.

By now, the original *Brighter Post Offices* project had already expanded into a quest for a proper *House Style* for Post Offices. As the incumbent advisor, Stuart Rose did not really welcome another person to give opinions on typography, and Henrion, as an outsider, sadly did not command the respect among the established department heads, or the PO Board.

Henrion's survey of the Post Office's image and branding came after the new *House Style* for public offices had been formalised and partway through the commissioning of the next telephone kiosk (the K8). It could be said that Henrion unnecessarily interfered with the choice of shade for the new standard PO red. Conversely, Henrion put in many hours of work attempting to understand the hierarchy of the business.

David Wainwright: *"The Henrion office now has a coordinated-indexed library of about 1,650 cards covering some 450 items, and about 120 people who control these items; and when completed this will form the 'fact storage' unit of any Post Office design brief."*

David Cabianca: *"Henrion accounts for his fee by recording 3036 hours invoiced, 668 hours not invoiced, and 198 meetings with records of the persons present at the respective meetings."*

With Hindsight

In 1967, the origin of this 'new red' transom bar was questioned. An internal memo to the MD of Postal operations explains how the colour was inadvertently introduced!

"There appears to be no documentation dealing specifically with the decision to use the new colour. The background is that we asked Mr. Bedford [Ministry of Public Buildings & Works architect and designer of PO Tower] in 1962 to design a house-style for Public Offices, drawing on the best of the features of schemes by MPB & W and two firms of consultants commissioned to modernise six of our more old-fashioned offices. One of the items we mentioned as probably warranting inclusion was a transom bar. The house-style design that Mr. Bedford produced included a transom bar in the new colour. His design, including the new colour, was put on exhibition at Fleet Building in mid-1962 and was generally well received by the then Assistant Postmaster General and members of the General Directorate. (The exhibition was shown to the Press later in the same year.)" H.A. DANIELS 27 July 1967.

This memo typically demonstrates the uncoordinated and sometimes confusing communication between the many different departments of the GPO. In practice the story was more complex, being a deliberate attempt by the GPO to produce a consistent image across its brand, albeit somewhat thwarted by contradictory opinions in a vast organisation. The new shade red had been agreed at Board level and was to be used in the next design of telephone kiosk.

K8 Kiosk

"The Post Office Board's approval of the introduction of a modern house-style for new public offices has established a recognition symbol which ought, if possible, to be reflected in the modern kiosk." [DDG memo to Board Feb 1965.]

At a meeting on 5 March 1965, the Board agreed that two new kiosk designs should be obtained. Mr. Douglas Scott FSIA and Mr. Bruce Martin FRIBA were both invited to submit sketches on the advice of Mr Henrion and the CoID. Mr Conder, who produced the K7 design in 1958, preferred not to submit further plans. Incidentally, Douglas Scott had already designed the pay-on-answer coinbox which enabled Subscriber Trunk Dialling (STD) in telephone kiosks.

Styling the Post Office

A GPO Press & Broadcast Notice of 13 July 1966 confirmed that the Post Office was developing a new telephone kiosk with Bruce Martin. The kiosk was to be painted in the *new standard* Post Office red.

18 June 1965 *"Mr Henrion explained that the adoption of the House Style as a standard future Post Office design was still very much in the air and far from final agreement."*

However, the concepts of House Style were already quite well-defined. *"Colour: The House Style for public offices uses in its transom bar the orange-red colour (BS 005) recommended by Casson and Black. Lettering: The lettering which will appear on the frontage and inside House Style offices will be in the [Clarendon] alphabet designed by Mr. Stuart Rose, under PRD [Public Relations Department] auspices, for General Post Office use."* [M.O. Tinniswood 30 September 1965.]

To clarify, the *House Style* colour of orange-red was British Standard BS 2660 range, shade 0-005 which under BS381C was No. 536, Poppy Red. Thus, it was intended to paint the K8 in Poppy Red. [Henrion's paperwork quoted No. 537 in error.]

On 7 Nov 1966 the Lion Foundry, Kirkintilloch, Glasgow was contracted to manufacture and supply six prototype kiosk No. 8s. The first of these was installed at 6-7 Old Palace Yard [House of Commons], Westminster on 12 July 1968.

Meanwhile, Henrion had been pursuing the possibility of distinctly separate colour identities for the proposed new divisions of the business e.g., yellow for telecommunications. This prompted much memo writing, and certainly some concern from the designer, Bruce Martin not least because red telephone kiosks were sacrosanct! At the beginning of 1968, the Board was also still open to suggestions for the exact shade of red to be used within postal.

Colour of Kiosk No. 8 (memo)

1.   A feature of the design of the kiosk No.8, designed by Bruce Martin, was a rather brighter red than that at present used for our kiosks. This design of kiosk was approved by the (then) PMG (Mr. Wedgwood-Benn) with the concurrence of Mr. Henrion – it is assumed that this approval included the colour. Bruce Martin has recently expressed great concern that he had not been consulted about a rumoured change of colour.

2.   Following the PO Board decision to defer a decision on "house" colour, the question of the choice of red for the Kiosk No.8 was discussed with DSS. He agreed that we should continue as originally intended and the Kiosk No.8 would be repainted in the colour recommended by Bruce Martin. Would you please arrange

accordingly. No change will, for the present, be made to the colour of the No.6 Kiosk. Kiosks No.6 and No.8 should not be erected adjacently.

3.   Would you please advise Mr. Bruce Martin and the Hon. Godfrey Samuel of the Royal Fine Art Commission that we shall continue, for the present, to paint kiosks red except where other colours are used in special places. [W.H. Maddison 15 May 1968.]

It was a strange idea to think that new and existing kiosks might be painted in different shades of red, but the exact shade was the subject of further discussion, while the Board still dithered over the possibility of yellow kiosks, which they knew the public wouldn't accept!

August 1968: Colour of Telephone Kiosks (memo)

The new K8 telephone kiosk now in use outside this building [PO HQ] and elsewhere is in the originally planned house style red. This was always the intention of the design project and was included in the design specification. Thus, the models which the PMG (Mr. Wedgwood Benn) and APMG [Assistant PMG] inspected, with you and Mr Henrion, in May 1966, were in this colour and there was no thought of anything different until the recent proposal to paint kiosks in yellow. Following the PO Board decision to defer the question of house colour (and later to retain yellow only for telecommunications vehicles), I agreed that we should continue with our original intention and have the Kiosk No.8 in house style red. This is a lighter red than the traditional Post Office red.

1. We are now ready to call off the first thousand production No.8 kiosks. It has just come to light, quite accidentally, that Mr. Mason decided at a presentation of colours on 9 May, that a shade of red (somewhat intermediate between the two reds and known as Cadmium 305) should replace house style red and the traditional PO red on the postal side. This at once raises the question what colour to paint the new kiosks, and there is a special difficulty that there is not yet a British Standard of this colour.

2. It could be argued that the juxtaposition of two different reds on a new kiosk and a re-painted pillar box would be ludicrous. The public would see it as change for change's sake. On the other hand, there is not a great difference between the shades of house style red and Cadmium 305, and such difference might be attributed to differences in painting and cleaning dates. We have no plans at present to re-paint existing kiosks in house style red and we would justify the new red on design grounds and the retention of Post Office red for existing kiosks on economy grounds. We shall, as it is, have green cabinets, concrete pillars, telecoms. vehicles eventually yellow, and with such a

kaleidoscope of colour, three different shades of red are little worse than two. I would therefore advocate continuing with the house style red for the production of new kiosks and with Post Office red for existing kiosks, at least for the time being. If, however, you wish to reconsider this, a specimen board in Cadmium 305 is available which you can see against a kiosk in house style red. Enclosed are samples of the three colours. [F. E. Jones 9 August 1968.]

J.D. Cartwright 23 September 1968: *It has been decided that the* **production** *run of Kiosks No. 8 should not be painted in 'House Style Red' but in a new shade of red now described as a monoazo pigment, Colour Index Reference C1 Pigment 9. Would you please inform Lion Foundry Co. Ltd.*

Memo from G. McMorran 20 August 1968: *"It seems to us that as both the postal and telecomms. businesses will be starting to use a new paint on a large scale there would be logic and economy in both sides using the same colour if practicable. We hope, therefore, that THQ would be prepared to consider using the new postal services red for kiosks."*

In an organisation as vast as the Post Office, small changes in corporate image could often have far reaching consequences, in terms of cost and brand integrity. Certainly, in later years more focus was given to coordinating design across the company.

Design Adviser

Henrion's initial design investigations during 1965 led to him being contracted up to mid-December 1967. He questioned whether Poppy Red would be a suitable paint pigment to effectively apply across all materials in the new Post Office corporation, for which he had already suggested some radical ideas both for business names and colour sets.

MEMORANDUM ON CHOICE AND STANDARDISATION OF PO CORPORATION RED by Henrion Design Associates 17th October 1967

Since our July presentation of proposals for identification for Posts and Telecoms, to members of the Board, we have gone into this matter in some depth. As a result, we shall shortly have ready a new presentation on Corporation Red.

The conclusions of our study are summarised below.

Saga of Postal Services Red

TWO PROBLEMS

There are two distinct problems: one is to choose a suitable red for the Corporation; the other is to standardise the chosen red. The natural first approach is to consider the BSI colours.

BSI COLOURS

BSI produce several standards in the colour field. The most important are BS 2660 'Colours for Building and Decorative Paints' and BS 381C 'Colours for Specific Purposes'.

The BSI colours are not a satisfactory basis for either choosing or standardising a red, for two main reasons.

The first reason is that the BSI colours offer too limited a choice. Both standards contain but two strong reds. One is the traditional PO Red BS 381C, colour 538; BS 2660, colour 0-006
The other is the MoPBW Poppy Red BS 381C, colour 536; BS 2660, colour 0-005. [House-style red] BS 381C additionally has one strong orange.
Poppy Red was shown at a previous presentation, including an actual vehicle and a telephone kiosk in this colour. It was agreed that it has an undesirable 'salmon' appearance, especially in large areas. Test and Inspection Branch have produced a series of 5% mixtures of PO Red and Poppy Red, which demonstrates that this effect is not overcome by such mixtures.

The second reason is that the BSI colours are simply colour samples without any pigment formulation. A colour sample can be matched by a variety of pigment mixtures, which may be very different in cost and permanence, and may not match the standard under different lighting and viewing conditions. Further, the BS 2660 samples are matt, while the BS 381C samples are glossy. Matching from matt to glossy is fundamentally unsatisfactory, involving colour changes equivalent to addition of significant quantities of white. Again, the BSI samples can vary from batch to batch. While adequate for many general purposes, the BSI colours cannot provide the precision of specification required by the Post Office.

A PROPOSED BASIS FOR CHOICE

We suggest that a more satisfactory approach is by considering pigments from the outset. It is true that the quality of a colour changes according to the material in which it is embodied, the light in which it is viewed (daylight, fluorescent, tungsten, sodium, mercury), and subjectively according to the size and surroundings of the sample. Such variations are minimised by using a single pigment throughout.
On the other hand, it is, as Mr Daniels notes, easy to be led into niceties of discrimination which are quite unnecessary. One of the most striking characteristics of human colour vision is its power to compensate for

varying viewing conditions. The apparent "changes" of colour under different viewing conditions only emerge in the highly artificial situation of concentrating attention on a colour sample, or of comparing two samples. The normal level of colour awareness and discrimination is low. It is perhaps only where two compounds butt together, as for example in a telephone handset, that close subjective matching is of much practical significance. In most situations, it is more important to ensure that pigments of suitable stability and cost are used.

The technical aspects of colour standardisation are complex. We have produced samples of pigments which we believe will satisfy all the technical requirements. Members of the Board are invited to choose a suitable colour from this range.

RED PIGMENTS
There are several chemical groups of red pigments which are commercially available:
Organic- azos, cinquazias, perylenes. Inorganic -cadmiums. These have various colour qualities, fastness to light, heat, and media, and costs.

COLOUR QUALITIES. Organics tend to have a bluish undertone, inorganics a yellowish undertone. For paints, considerable quantities of white are necessary to give the required opacity. The paint then has to be coloured by a pigment. The staining power of a pigment is therefore important for paints, since there is a limit to the loading which a medium can take. Some of the organics are strong strainers requiring only some 6 oz per gallon; while the cadmiums are weaker strainers, requiring only some 4 Ib per gallon, and hence may cost more for paint of a required strength of colour.

FASTNESS TO LIGHT. The cadmiums are very good. Many of the organics are poor, except for some of the more expensive.

FASTNESS TO HEAT. Fore thermo-plastics and vitreous stove enamelling, fastness to heat is essential. All the organics are poor, while the cadmiums are very good.

FASTNESS TO MEDIA. The different pigments have very varied properties in different media. For example, spraying paints include xylol, in which organic pigments bleed and lose gloss.

MIXING PROPERTIES. The cadmiums are hard pigments, difficult to grind, and they tend to settle or float out from paint media. Most organic pigments mix far more easily.

Saga of Postal Services Red

MATCHING. There is little difficulty in initial matching of colours between the various pigments. Difficulties arise from the different behaviours of initially matched colours over long periods and in different media. Colours which are satisfactory in paints and plastics can be matched without difficulty in printing inks.

DISCUSSION. Cadmium pigments are unsurpassed for stability to heat and light. There is a wide range of cadmiums, from yellows to deep reds, affording ample choice. A cadmium pigment would be very suitable for defining a colour, and for making standard samples of great permanence. In processes involving heat, a cadmium pigment would be specified. On the other hand, there are many situations where lower permanence is acceptable, and where cost is an overriding consideration. There is hence a need for pigment formulations matching the cadmium standard, using organics suitable for the various media.

PRESENTATION. We have, with the help of Test and Inspection Branch, James M. Brown Limited, and Postans Limited, prepared paint samples of two pure cadmium pigments (James M. Brown references 305 and 306), and a 1:1 mixture of the two. ED/I and Postans Limited have also prepared paint samples of two pure organic diazo pigments which are fairly good matches to the cadmiums (chlorinated para red 4586, matching cadmium 305; bon arylamide red 4655, matching cadmium 3.6), and a 1:1 mixture. In each case the medium is the same as that used for many years for Post Office paints. There is no technical difficulty about varying the proportions of the mixtures of either cadmium or diazo pigments. The cost of the cadmium pigments is about 10/- per Ib, and that of the diazo pigments is about 11/- per Ib. However, paint requires 3 to 4 Ib per gallon of cadmium, 5 to 8 oz per gallon of diazo. The pigment cost of paints per gallon is thus some 35/- for cadmium, 5/- for diazo. The presentation will include, as well as the above:

BS 381C, colour 538 traditional Post Office Red
BC 381C colour 536: Poppy Red

BS 2660, colour 0-006: matt correlate to Post Office Red
BS 2660, colour 0-005: matt correlate to Poppy Red

ED/I match to BS 2660 0-006
ED/I match to BS 2660 0-005

Mixtures of Poppy Red with 5, 10, 15, 20, 25, 30, 40, and 50% Post Office Red.

RECOMMENDATION
Choose one of the cadmium pigments to be shown at the presentation as a basic standard. Lay down matching formulations in organic pigments for brushing paint, spraying paint, and any other media where lower standards of permanence are acceptable, or where cost is an overriding factor.

Test and Inspection Branch are in full support of this recommendation. We hope by this approach to bring rational considerations into the choice of a standard colour, and to remove the main basis for decision from the purely subjective field. We also hope to minimise the variations and complications at present caused by a great number of uncontrolled pigment formulations in various media.

H. A. Daniels 30 October 1967: *"It will be interesting to see Mr. Henrion's demonstration. His approach to the subject seems needlessly involved, and some of his colour descriptions are wrong."*

A meeting to consider further a new red for Posts 11th Jan 1968: *"Four hardboard panels painted in different reds, and three small postal vans painted in cadmium paints 305 (dark red) 306 (orange red) and a 1:1 mix of 305 and 306, were seen. The PMG had favoured the 1:1 mix for postal vans when he saw them on 16th November 1967. Mr. Wolstencroft had earlier favoured red 305. The purpose of the meeting was to recommend a red which would do for all purposes. It was agreed that only colours 305 and the 1:1 mix should be recommended to the PO Board, and before going ahead the small postal vans in these colours, and two letter boxes, one per colour, should be seen side by side."*

The meeting with the PMG to see the postal vans and letter boxes took place on 9 May 1968 (HQ Building, Room G6, for letter boxes, HQ courtyard for the vans).

Implementation
F.E. Jones 9 August 1968: *"Mr Mason decided at a presentation of colours on 9th May [1968], that a new red (known as Cadmium 305) intermediate between the former "house" colour and traditional red should be used on the Postal side. This raises again the question of the colour of the new kiosks, of which we are now ready to call off the first thousand. There is an added difficulty as there is not yet a British Standard for the new colour. It could be argued that the permanent juxtaposition of different reds on a kiosk and a pillar box would be ludicrous."*

Painting of Kiosks and Letter Boxes
24 Oct 1968 "...the painting of kiosks is still the responsibility of HPs [Head Postmasters] – it will be some time before it is transferred to TMs [Telephone Managers]. The work in respect kiosks, letterboxes and stamp selling machines should be arranged as one job under one contract in each locality. It would be appropriate for PHQ [postal HQ] to issue an instruction to DPRs which could be agreed by THQ [Telecom HQ] insofar as kiosks are concerned."

Saga of Postal Services Red

Circular 31 July 1969:

PHQ Circular 179/69 and THQ Circular 261/69
To: PHQ Depts (partial); D/PRs; HPmrs and DPmrs; THG Deps (partial)

POSTAL SERVICE RED

1. There are two shades of red currently in use in the Post Office;
BS 2660 0-006 as used on street letter boxes and OMVs [Own motor vehicles] and a more vivid shade,
BS 2660 0-005 as used on public office house style signs and transom bars.
There would be an obvious advantage in having a single shade for all purposes, and one has been selected. This Circular gives details of the method and timescale for introducing this shade which should henceforth be regarded as standard.

2. The standard shade, which should be referred to as Postal Service Red, is between and visually reasonably close to 0-005 and 0-006. We have applied for its inclusion in the BS series. It will be introduced gradually, as practical circumstances permit, for all items in the postal business where red is now used. THQ have agreed that it will also be used on telephone kiosks.

3. STREET LETTER BOXES, STAMP SELLING MACHINE CASES AND TELEPHONE KIOSKS

    New telephone kiosks are being provided in the standard shade of red. New letter boxes etc. will be provided in the standard shade as soon as practicable. Existing letter boxes, kiosks etc. should be changed to Postal Service Red on normal maintenance repainting. Existing stocks of red paint held by local painting contractors should be used up as far as possible before introducing Postal Service Red. New rectangular posting boxes have a special finish; normal local repainting procedures do not apply to these boxes and special arrangements will be made as necessary under the direction of PMD/DD.
    3.1 Apart from normal maintenance repainting, arrangements should be made when Postal Service Red paint is available for repainting in this shade:-

3.1.1 any street letter box in close visual proximity to a telephone kiosk which is in the standard shade and the colour difference could invite criticism;
3.1.2 any pillar type letter box on which the new stamp machine case type "U" (which will be in the standard shade) has been mounted or is expected to be mounted shortly;
3.1.3 any telephone kiosk in close visual proximity to a street letter box in the standard shade.

3.2 Painting specifications should be amended in manuscript pending reprint.

4. Postal Fleet
New vehicles will ultimately be provided in the standard shade. Existing vehicles should be repainted in Postal Service Red as they become due for repainting.

5. Cycles
New cycles will be provided in the standard shade as soon as practicable. Re-enamelling of cycles is not normally justified (see Rg 29 V 3) but where re-enamelling is authorised the standard shade should be specified.

6. Uniform Badges (metal and cloth) which incorporate red
No action will be taken on existing stocks. The red in future stocks will however match Postal Service Red as far as is practicable.

7. The first supplies of Postal Service Red paint are now available and should be requisitioned.

8. Colour match standards and full details of the standard shade may be obtained from Mr. L. E Terrett, THQ Purchasing and Supplies Department, P & S 4.3, London Materials Section, Studd Street, London, N.1. (Telephone 01-226 1262 Extn. 333).

9. Publicity
No publicity is being given to the introduction of a standard shade, but if questions are received, they should be answered factually on the basis of the information in paras. 1 and 2 above.

10. This Circular is issued for action in the postal business: THQ are issuing a separate instruction. Enquiries should be addressed via RDs to Mr. E. W. O'Connor, PHQ/PMD/EB 2.2 (01-432 5740).

11. This Circular should be cancelled on 31st July 1971 unless it has been cancelled earlier.

BS/AT/101 L.T. WOOD

Saga of Postal Services Red

Memos Arising

G.H. Coates 4 August 1969: *"I am still seeing postal service red after receiving PHQ Circular 179/69 (THQ Circular 261/79) this morning. Who on earth decided to call the new colour 'postal service red' rather than 'Post Office red,' which would be much more appropriate? Logically, as the paint is to be applied also to telephone kiosks it might equally well be called telephone service red. The general public and paint decorators will almost certainly call the new colour Post Office red. Why can't we accept this and be sensible?"*

8 August 1969 G. McMorran: *"We should have liked to call the new colour Post Office Red, but this had already been pre-empted by a BSI standard colour, BS2660 0-006. As the new colour is not the same as BS2660 0-006 we had no option but to find another name for it."*

20 August 1969 GL Thomasson: *"PHQ has decided to adopt as the distinctive colour for the Postal Service a red which is an intermediate shade between PO Red BS 0-006 (used on street letter boxes etc.) and the brighter red BS 0-005 (used on public office house styles transom bars). The new red, which is to be known as 'Postal Service Red' will be used on all items in postal business on which red is now used."*

28 November 1969 WH Maddison: *"The first deliveries of Kiosks No.8 were in the house red, but for practical reasons is now being replaced by the new 'Postal Service Red'."*

New British Standards

Circa 1988 British Standards did a review of paint colours under BS381C. The names of four of the colours were changed as they were considered no longer appropriate, thus 267 *Traffic Green* became 267 *Deep Chrome Green*; 368 *Traffic Yellow* became 568 *Apricot*.

538 *Post Office Red* became 538 *Cherry*

539 *Postal Service Red* became 539 *Currant Red*

Postscript

The Post Office Board was in a difficult position at the impending launch of the new 'standard red' K8 telephone kiosk. The kiosk colour was expected to match the modern house style of public offices which had started design in the early 1960s. This coincided with proposals for a separate identity for telecommunications, which for the foreseeable future was still to remain a part of the Post Office. It may have been sensible to go for an all-yellow identity for telecommunications rather than the choice actually made of only painting vans yellow for safety reasons. In any case, both the K8 designer and the general public would not at that time have tolerated anything other than red for kiosks. In choosing the final shade for House Style, the implications of having a disparity of reds between pillar boxes and kiosks should have been considered at the outset. The lack of joined-up thinking across the Post Office most certainly delayed the implementation of a modern corporate image. Henrion's ideas of distinctly separate trading-unit colours were otherwise sound, but some of his associated thinking was clearly not appropriate for the Post Office. Ultimately, he was defeated by the whole lack of coordination that was the PO hierarchy.

In Final Summary

Post Office Red 538 was the original colour of post-boxes and telephone kiosks.

Poppy Red 536 was the *House Style* transom bar and hanging-sign colour and also the colour in which the K8 kiosk (pre-production run) was first painted.

The previously unnamed colour, *Cadmium 305* became *Postal Services Red 539* and was the new colour (eventually) adopted across both the telecoms and postal businesses.

BS 2660, colour 0-006: matt correlate to Post Office Red
BS 2660, colour 0-005: matt correlate to Poppy Red

The accuracy of colour reproduction cannot be guaranteed, but these samples held by BT Archives show:

Left: Post Office red [538]
Right: Cadmium 305 red [539]

6.2: Telephone Kiosks

A brief look at standard GPO telephone kiosks No.1 to No. 8.
In 1912 as the GPO became the monopoly supplier of telecommunications in the UK, it inherited many 'silence-cabinets' and telephone kiosks which had previously been the responsibility of the National Telephone Company (NTC). The GPO didn't have a standard design of its own, and the question arose as to what colour kiosks should be?

Telephone Kiosks, Repainting

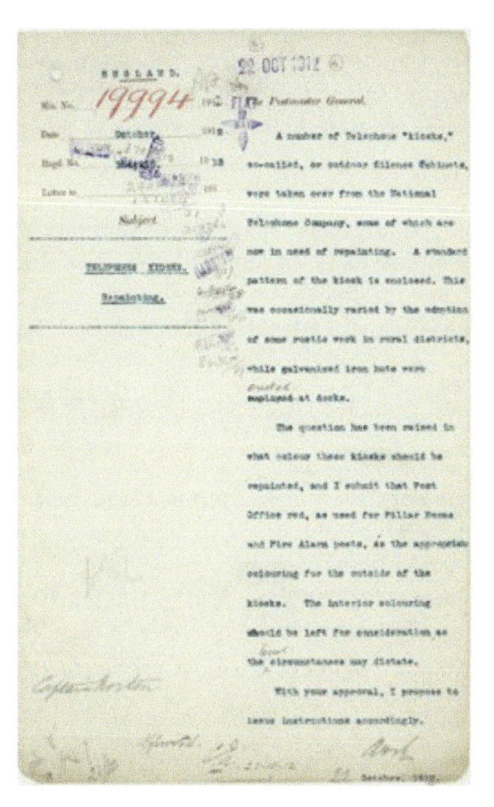

Minute No. 19994 dated 22 October 1912.
The Postmaster-General

*Several Telephone "kiosks," so-called, or Silence Cabinets, were taken over from the National Telephone Company, some of which are now in need of repainting. A standard pattern of the kiosk is enclosed. This was occasionally varied by the adoption of some rustic work in rural districts, which galvanised iron huts were erected at docks. The question has been raised in what colour these kiosks should be repainted, and **I submit that Post Office red, as used for Pillar Boxes and Fire Alarm posts, is the appropriate colouring for the outside of the kiosks.** The interior colouring should be left for consideration, as the local circumstances may dictate. With your approval, I propose to issue instructions accordingly.*

Having confirmed the choice of red, the Post Office then commissioned its first standard design of kiosk which was predominantly a concrete structure that didn't warrant a painted finish!

Repainting

"Kiosks No. 1 are moulded with fine artificial stone finish and apart from the difficulty of obtaining a satisfactory paint present a much better appearance unpainted. Every endeavour should therefore be made to induce Local Authorities to allow the Kiosks to remain unpainted." [Extract from Engineering Monthly List February 1923.]

"Kiosks will be provided, painted, and maintained by the Engineering Department as a general rule. They can be painted any desired colour or colours to meet local conditions, but the painting of concrete kiosks should not be encouraged. The Engineer should be informed what colour is required." [Extract from Service Instructions G3 Para 20 November 1923.] For example, the Sectional Engineer's report of July 1929: "…these [K1] kiosks at present are painted *Middle Brunswick Green* as originally requested by the Liverpool Council."

In order to improve the appearance of Kiosk No.1 all kiosks of this type in which the concrete has not previously been painted should be specially treated as described below. The concrete surface inside and out will be coated and stippled with 'Cantex Stipple paint No.3' The window frames together with the beadings and the whole of the door should be painted with Hadfields Paint Heolin red finish. [Amendment to Circular Telephones 351 February 1923.]

"Stipple paint is a special composition which has a consistency somewhat greater than that of ordinary paint and which, being quick drying, sets fairly hard within twenty-four hours of being applied and continues to harden with time. A rougher finish should be given to those portions of the interior surface that are subject to pencilling on the part of the public." [POED Technical Instructions XXXVI Call Office Installations Part 3 Kiosks August 1931.]

Kiosk Paint Summary

K1 and K3 paint: Stipple; Primer; Undercoat; Finishing, *Special Red*. Varnish: Weatherproof. *Oxide Red* for the metal window frames.
K2 and K4: Interior *Flame* coloured finishing paint. Exterior *Special Red* finishing paint.
Essentially, all kiosks had a *Special Red* exterior, which as a BSI paint was *Post Office Red* by the time the K6 went into production. The K8 introduced *Postal Service Red*, a new shade.

Letter Boxes

In 1927 pure *Vermilion* was specified for the painting of Pillar, Wall, and Lamp letter boxes, as manufactured, but *Post Office Red* was found to be superior, and it was recommended that the specification be changed. [POST 78/301]

Concrete Kiosks: K1 and K3

Left: K1 kiosk.

Right: K3 kiosk.

Concrete kiosks K1 at Amberley Museum (2008) and K3 at Science Museum, London (2000). Photos © J. Chenery.

Styling the Post Office

Giles Gilbert Scott's **K3** went into production in 1929 and for a while it was the standard kiosk for sites outside of London. However, the concrete fabrications were both difficult to transport and did not weather well.

Street Box Fire Alarms
These metal boxes were mounted on pillars at strategic points in towns.

For Fire: Break glass. Pull down lever. Wait for engine.

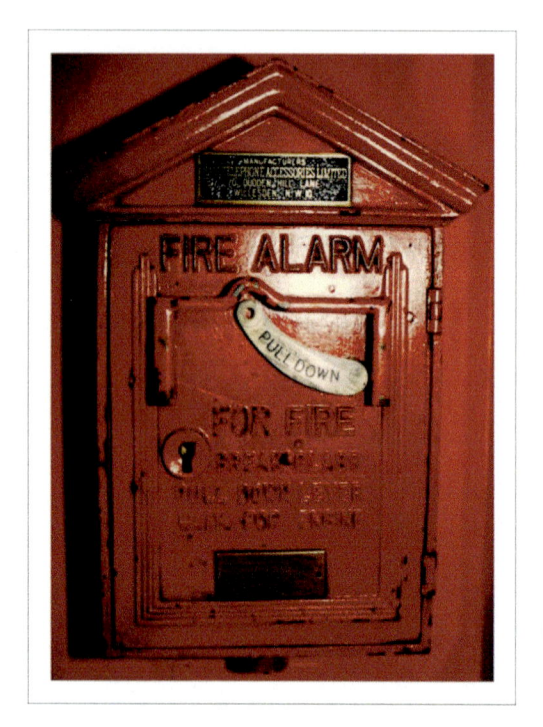

"...I submit that Post Office red, as used for Pillar Boxes and Fire Alarm posts, is the appropriate colouring for the outside of the kiosks."

These red fire alarm street boxes were made for the GPO by Hall Telephone Accessories (HTA) Ltd, who also made the A & B coinboxes for telephone kiosks.

HTA was later known as Associated Automation at 70 Dudden Hill Lane, Willesden, London, NW10.

Photo: Fire Alarm Street Box at Telecom Technology Showcase © Laurence Rudolf.

"These were first installed in 1880, normally positioned on pavements at street corners where they could easily be seen. They were connected directly by landline to the local fire station. When activated by the caller, the alarm bell sounded in the fire station and the location of the alarm sounded was indicated."
[Extract from london-fire.gov.uk/museum/history-and-stories/communications-in-london-fire-brigade/]

K2: A Kiosk for the Provinces

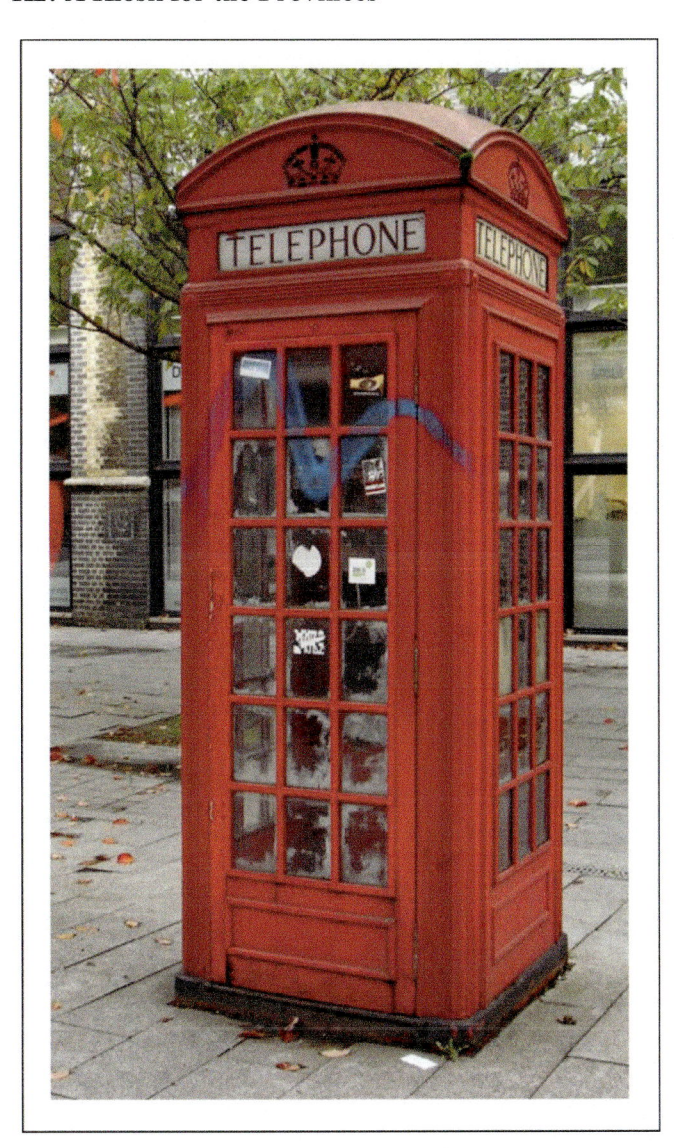

The K2 was designed by Giles Gilbert Scott and was fabricated in cast iron. Its uniform pattern of oblong panes of glass instantly distinguishes it from the later K6.

The K2 and K4 kiosks were originally specified to have *Flame* (red) paint internally, and *Special Red* externally.

In its heyday the K2 was a prestigious, functional piece of street furniture, a befitting representation of the Post Office, large, solid, and everlasting.

Justification for a K2: The architectural surroundings call for a more ornamental design than those of Nos. 1 or 3.

In later times, kiosks were more of a target for vandalism, use as toilets, and an advertising haven for prostitutes' calling cards. Smoke ridden kiosks, with discarded cigarette-ends, were not a place to linger. Infrequently used, some became rubbish tips, while still their iconic significance was celebrated and cherished.

Left: K2 in London © J. Chenery (2014).

Technical Instruction XXXVI (August 1931):
"In no circumstances should kiosks be allowed to have a dilapidated appearance."

K4: Telephone and Stamp Vending in cast iron.

K4 kiosk at Amberley Museum © J. Chenery (2008). Below: Stamp machines and letter box incorporated into the kiosk. Note the G R (George V) inscription. Stamps were ½ d (less than one new penny).

The **K5** used an improved concrete moulding of the K3 design which was more suitable for volume production. However, this was superseded by the K6 before manufacture began.

Decoration of Telephone Kiosks Specification T543G (1960)
Kiosks Nos. 1 and 3: The glazing frames in the door and sides of the kiosk and, in Kiosk No.1, the wood door frame shall be painted one coat of 'Paint, Glossy P.O. Red.'
Kiosks Nos. 2, 4 and 6: The remainder of the internal surfaces, excluding the concrete floor, but including the conduits, cables and electric light fittings, and the whole of the external surfaces shall be painted one coat of 'Paint, Glossy P.O. Red.'

Telephone Kiosks

K6: The Jubilee Kiosk in cast iron.

Giles Gilbert Scott's K6 adorned many a post office, and street corner in the days when home telephones were still a luxury item. *British Standard* paint colours were introduced in 1930 and were adopted mainly by government departments, the service industry, and the military. Consequently, the **K6** Jubilee Kiosk of 1936 was specified to be finished in ***Post Office Red*** to BS381 shade no. 38 (later 538). In 1948 the scheme was revised as BS381C.

> *"The primary reason for choosing Post Office red is that a kiosk must be readily distinguishable from its surroundings so as to be recognised from a distance by a stranger in the stress of an emergency and uniformity of colour is essential if this object is to be achieved."*
> [Telephone Service Instructions G3 March 1960.]

The ubiquitous K6 Jubilee kiosk at Market Hill, Cambridge © Malcolm Jones (2011)

K7: See 'Brighter Post Offices' chapter 5.1

K8: A Modern Style for New Towns

Bruce Martin's strikingly modern design included large, glazed panes. This kiosk was fabricated in cast iron but with a cast aluminium door, and was manufactured by Lion Foundry of Kirkintilloch, near Glasgow.

One of the six trial K8s was sited by the west gate of Post Office HQ, GPO North, King Edward Street, London, with the telephone number 01-606 5971X during July 1968.

Trial batches of the K8 kiosk were finished in *House Style* (*Poppy Red* 536) as originally intended by Bruce Martin. However, for the production run the colour was matched to the new corporate shade of *Postal Service Red* BS 381C No. 539. [This new shade of red was confirmed in THQ Circular 227/69 7 July 1969.]

The coinbox (payphone) mechanism with integral handset and dial supported the rollout of STD (Subscriber Trunk Dialling) which had begun in 1958.

K8 at Milton Keynes Museum © J. Chenery (2014).

The K8 was the last kiosk to be produced in cast iron. A completely different build of kiosk was developed during the British Telecom era.

6.3: Post Office Red

"There is one primary colour to which the Post Office has established a definite and indefeasible claim- the red of the letter box and the mail van."
[Ref: Brigadier-General Sir Frederic Williamson, Director of Postal Services - Post Office Magazine Jan 1934.]

The origins of Royal Mail date back to 1516 with the appointment of Sir Brian Tuke as Master of the Posts.

Transportation of the mail between towns used contractors' coaches and horses.
The colour schemes were generally applied as a black upper, the doors and wheels as maroon or red.

The General Post Office Act of 1660 formerly recognised the Post Office and the appointment of a Postmaster-General.

From 1787 the Post Office adopted an improved design of 'patent coach' from London builder John Besant.

Mail coaches at The Postal Museum (top) and the Science Museum (right) © J. Chenery (2019).

Uniforms

The colour of the mail coach wheels is said to have been the origin of *Post Office Red* paint.

"Post Office Red has been standard since 1799, when it was introduced for mail coaches instead of the old black and maroon, though postboys had been dressed in it earlier." [Post Office Magazine Jan 1961.]

In 1784 the first Royal Mail uniform for its coach guards was issued.

A gold braided scarlet coat with blue lapels was matched with a black hat ringed with a gold band.

Note in the display case, the pistols that the guard was issued with to safeguard the journey of the mail from highwaymen.

Between c1859 and July 1874, street pillar boxes were painted green, until the more conspicuous red was adopted.

Display case at The Postal Museum © J. Chenery (2017).

Post Office Red

Street Furniture: Pillar Boxes

In 1866 the first design of Penfold box was both practical and ornate.

From July 1874 the red colour was adopted as standard, in place of the former dark green, and the Penfold was the first box to be painted in this new colour.

Post Boxes from about 1887 onwards included the name POST OFFICE as part of the casting.

Finally, for new castings circa 1991 onwards the words POST OFFICE have been superseded with ROYAL MAIL.

Left: Penfold pillar box (replica). Right: A modern 'Royal Mail' box. Seen at Debden store © J. Chenery (2014).

Departments of the Post Office

As the long-established (General) Post Office organised its departments during the 1900s there was already a natural separation of functions, typically between postal, and telegraph/telephone activities, and this split ultimately influenced the design of its motor vehicle fleets and identities. Conversely, shared premises for telephone exchanges and post offices was very convenient, and possible due to single ownership. The GPO umbrella covered both businesses. The Stores Department delivered furniture to post offices and engineering departments alike. Bulk purchasing across business functions was advantageous.

The Post Office was a vast organisation to administer (over 358,000 staff in 1959). Each department tended to be very compartmentalised and consequently co-ordination across the business was lacking. Growth in functions developed in a haphazard manner which inevitably led to departments having distinctive identities which failed to project a joined-up corporate identity.

As the 1960s progressed, the Post Office sought a single corporate image but with a pronounced separation of businesses as it reorganised in preparation for Corporation status. And by 1975 just as this co-ordinated identity was finally realised in practice, the businesses were gearing up for ultimate separation with the demerger of British Telecom and subsequent privatisation.
Throughout, badging of vehicles closely followed the organisational structure of the Post Office.

Motor Vehicle Fleets: The Red Fleet

Stores Department

Within the GPO, Postal Stores and Stores Offices (Telegraphs) amalgamated in 1902 to form the Stores Department, and its own red vehicle fleet developed from 1906. In 1903 bicycles for postmen were sourced in this manner. Thus, the red stores fleet and the evolving red postal fleet were both managed by the Stores Controller's Mechanical Transport Section. Motor vehicles were supplied as authorised by The Secretary and issued to individual Head Postmasters. By 1919 the Stores Department had acquired several dozen heavy vehicles.

The Mechanical Transport Section of the Stores Department was transferred to the Engineer-in-Chief to become the Motor Transport Branch of the Engineering Department in a phased transfer between July and October 1931.

Post Office Red

A Contracts Department was formed on 1 April 1941, and a Factories Department (Fac. D) on 1 May. Birmingham was one key stores location where Fac. D was also based, manufacturing and refurbishing all manner of items, ranging from furniture, and switchboards to exchange equipment.

POST OFFICE STORES DEPARTMENT- BIRMINGHAM

A 1939 Scammell Rigid 6, drop side, 12 Ton lorry – GGH 252 © Lynda Bullock (2008).

The Stores Department was renamed Supplies Department on 4 November 1948 and continued to serve individual Section Stores etc. from its depots. Later as part of the Purchasing and Supplies Department, its red vehicles were repainted yellow, and lettered Supplies Division from autumn 1968.

Studd Street Stores (Islington)

John Tythe writes:

"The building in Studd Street, now known as 8 Esther Anne Place, was an engineering building, which housed the Engineer-in-Chief's Office; London Test Section and London Materials Section, and the main GPO Stores prior to its move to the Crayford depot, and also the GPO Factories Division until that part and those based in Bovay Place, Holloway, transferred to Bilton Way, Enfield."

Alldays and Onions 30cwt 1910 Stores Department vehicle G. P. O. Studd St. N showing the G R (George V) crown.

As a government department, GPO books, diaries and ledgers were supplied by the Stationery Office (S.O.) under contract and marked with the reigning monarch's crown. These were considered postal stores and held at Mount Pleasant, Clerkenwell.

Booklet scans from author's collection.

In later years Studd Street housed the Royal Mail Northern District Office (NDO) and MT (motor transport) workshop.

Cypher on Mailvans

Cypher updates followed the reigning monarchs: George V 1910-1936; Edward VIII 1936; George VI 1936-1952, and Elizabeth II 1952. Signwriting of lettering progressed from ROYAL MAIL in black, to gilt.

George V  *Elizabeth II*

Telegram Messengers

Mailvans were never badged GPO, but telegram messenger bikes were! The organisation of the Post Office had many contradictions. For example, at one time, telephonists were the responsibility of Head Postmasters.

> The transmission of telegrams belonged to the telecommunications side of the business, but the acceptance and delivery was a postal function.
>
> These were the sorts of sensible arrangements that had to be finally reconciled when the GPO later split into posts and telephones (PO/BT).

Telegram Messenger motorbikes in preservation, visiting Milton Keynes Museum © J. Chenery (2015).

Styling the Post Office

Mailvans
From 1953 new Royal Mail vans were consistently sign-written in gilt (golden) typeface.

Note the later ER cypher and St. Edward's crown. The cab door features the Post Office roundel, responsible Head Postmaster, and vehicle serial number.

A 1960s Morris JB type YLH 449 in preservation, visiting Milton Keynes Museum © J. Chenery (2014).

Post Office Red

Of Paint Colours

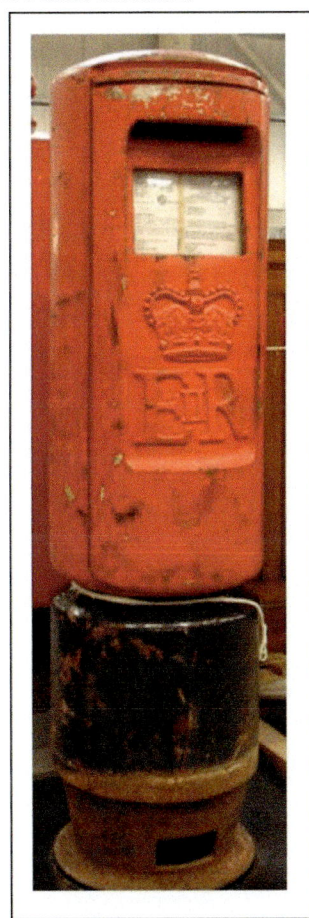

Before 1930, standard paint colours weren't formulated or matched as accurately as today.

In 1930 British Standards listed Post Office Red as shade No. 38, which became 538 in 1948 and remained the definitive shade in the GPO until 1968 when Postal Service Red 539 began to supersede it.

The Type K pillar box designed by Tony Gibbs was introduced in 1980.

Left: A modern Type K at Debden Store © J. Chenery (2014).

Right: A George VI box in the street © J. Chenery (2013).

A New Red

The long-established Post Office Red (538) changed shade prior to the organisation transitioning to a corporation. On 20 August 1969 G.L. Thomasson wrote:

"PHQ has decided to adopt as the distinctive colour for the Postal Service a red which is an intermediate shade between PO Red BS 0-006 (used on street letter boxes etc.) and the brighter red BS 0-005 (used on public office house styles transom bars). The new red, which is to be known as 'Postal Service Red' will be used on all items in postal business on which red is now used."

Postal Service Red was BS 381C No. 539. The shades 0-005 and 0-006 were categorised under BS 2660 (1955) Colours for Building and Decorative Paints.

The J4 Mailvan

Morris vans were a common sight on the streets during the 1960s. The final batch purchased by the Post Office was in 1974. Bedford HAs then became the commonplace small mailvan, as well as Leyland Sherpas.

A 1974 Austin Morris J4 PVE 438N in preservation, visiting Amberley Museum © Mark Skillen (2019). Note the advertising board on the van side, a feature of the analogue age, long before www.

From 1975 mailvans' liveries began to be supplied in the *Banks and Miles* design and lettering (chapter 10.2).

7: Mid-Bronze Green

British Standard Colour BS381C No. 223 Mid-Bronze Green.

The association of green paint with the General Post Office can be positively traced back to the late 1850s.

Letter Offices for the collection of post were being supplemented by street pillar boxes, which between c1859 and July 1874 were painted green. There is some conjecture as to the exact shade because modern-day paint standards, formulation, and accurate matching were not devised until c1930.

Across industry, shades evolved into Brunswick Green, Light Bronze Green, Mid-Bronze Green, and Deep Bronze Green.

Bronze-Green became a steadfast utilitarian colour, a popular finish for stationery steam engines, passenger trains, racing cars, and army vehicles.

However, for street furniture, green was unobtrusive, but pillar boxes needed to be easily located, hence the likely reason for the change to red from late 1874.

During the 1930s, vehicle liveries of *Mid-Bronze Green* telephone vans with white lettering defined and became the visible identity of the Post Office Telephones department. Road safety concerns prompted a phased change to *Golden Yellow* from 1968 coinciding with corporation status in 1969.

A green first national standard pillar box at Debden store © J. Chenery (2014).

GPO/POED/POT

The Post Office Engineering Department (POED) listed this paint as *Service Green*. At the start of the Post Office's telegraph/telephone monopoly (1912), hand carts for the erection of telegraph poles were marked G.P.O. (General Post Office). By the mid-1930s, Post Office Telephones was the preferred wording, for the telephone business (at least on vehicles), but the abbreviation GPO continued to be used across departments and media, and by the public, to denote the top hierarchical authority.

Specification, carts, pole (TL 18 formerly 228G) for the painting of handcarts:

"For the guidance of the contractor in obtaining the desired shade, a sample 1 lb. tin of Service Green paint will be supplied on application to The Controller, P.O. Stores Department."

A GPO handcart is adjacent to a Post Office Telephones linesman's van ELO 688 at Amberley Museum © J. Chenery (2010).

Mid-Bronze Green

Post Office Railway (London)

An electric underground railway, specifically designed to carry letters and small packets was opened by the Post Office in 1927. It ran from Paddington to Whitechapel connecting sorting offices and mainline rail stations. The rolling stock was finished in the same *Mid-Bronze Green* (Service Green) colour as the Post Office's engineering/telephone fleet.

Post Office Railway 1927

Although the railway carried Royal Mail items, the colour scheme was that of the Post Office Engineering Department - the drab *Service Green*. It did not need to be vibrant as the railway was neither visible to the public or much thought of as a marketing opportunity. Public service industries didn't need to compete for business!

By the mid-1980s co-ordinated branding, advertising, and filming to demonstrate efficiency and good service was one of the catalysts for rebranding as *Mail Rail* in 1987.

The railway used Royal Mail's colour scheme - the distinctive orange-red was BS 381C shade no.539 *Postal Service Red*.

A carriage/motive unit from the original POR seen at Debden © J. Chenery (2014).
Inset: A later motive unit after repainting to Postal Service Red.

After 60 years (1987) it was renamed *Mail Rail* and continued operating until 2003 by which time its mail-handling infrastructure had become outmoded, too costly, and sadly obsolescent.

Street Furniture

The GPO's cross-connexion cabinets, Primary Connection Points (PCPs) which gave flexibility in copper cabling distribution to telephone subscribers were also finished in *Mid-Bronze Green*.

Years of fading in the sun, together with many re-paints are particularly noticeable in these examples which appear to be *Brunswick Green*.

Above: A GPO (PCP) street cabinet.

Right: A PO marked (PCP) street cabinet.

Photos © J. Chenery (2007).

These older cabinets were cast iron; later ones were fabricated steel. Historically, cabinets never carried any real branding apart from the subtle markings GPO/PO/British Telecom/BT. This situation changed following the rollout circa 2010 of new co-located cabinets which were necessary to allow fibre broadband connections.

Broadband Cabinets

Installed by contractors for Openreach, the fibre broadband cabinets (Fibre to The Cabinet – FTTC product) essentially placed Digital Subscriber Line Analogue Multiplexer (DSLAM) equipment onto the street. This became high-profile in marketing the service because the appearance of the larger wardrobe-sized boxes was reasonable surety that the broadband product had arrived! However, some customers objected having these larger cabinets next to their garden walls where space on the pavement was at a premium. Posters on the cabinets proclaimed *"Fibre broadband is here"* to encourage internet customers to upgrade or be connected for the first time.

Below: A large DSLAM cabinet adjacent to a long-existing PCP © J. Chenery (2012).

The large cabinets are about 1.6 metres high.

Above: A small DSLAM cabinet © J. Chenery (2012).

Mobile Telephone Exchanges

From 1939, Mobile Automatic Exchanges, MAX 12 and 13s, were developed to provide additional switching capacity at locations where either accommodation or equipment was lacking. They were also provided to temporarily reinstate services following fire/flood or (wartime) bombings.

A MAX 13 comprised of two trailers. Section A with subscribers' equipment for 200 lines, and section B for junction equipment and power plant

Above: A MAX 13 No. 1004 section B, 1949 at Kidbrooke, courtesy of BT Group Archives. Ref: TCB 417/E 16238.

"Kidbrooke CRD (Central Repair Depot) undertakes the complete overhaul of heavy vehicles, motorcycles and mechanical aids employed in the London and Home Counties regions." [Commercial Motor Magazine December 1960.]

For an organisation as large as the GPO there was inherently much inconsistency of branding across business functions and departments. Updated branding was slow and costly to implement, and tended to lag behind trends, especially when repainting or re-badging of vehicle fleets was required.

Early MAX trailers were painted *Mid-Bronze Green* and finished with the GPO monogram (1934 version) in white, plus a T-series serial number to denote the particular trailer.
Further growth in demand for telephone service led to new MNDX (Mobile Non-Director Exchange) mobiles, from 1967 onwards, which allowed main exchange extensions, and easier working to the new STD (Subscriber Trunk Dialling).

Mid-Bronze Green

The New Mobiles

These new MNDX trailers were finished with the updated (1953) GPO monogram which incorporated the St. Edward's Crown, plus POST OFFICE TELEPHONES, TELEPHONE MANAGER.

MNDX No.127 and MAX12 No. 29 at Milton Keynes Museum © J. Chenery (2014).

In the 1970s trailers were also equipped with TXE2 electronic kit (designated MXE2) as the switching technology evolved. The *Mid-Bronze Green* colour was retained as these trailers were intended to be parked off-road and didn't need to be conspicuous. Only a few were known to be repainted in telecom [safety] *Golden Yellow*.

Styling the Post Office

POED Motor Transport

Within the Post Office Engineering Department, a motor transport scheme was established in 1919. POED utility vehicles retained the service green colour of GPO handcarts. This steadily growing fleet was liveried in *Mid-Bronze Green* and typically sign written with:

POST OFFICE ENGINEERING DEPARTMENT.

A 1932 Morris 12, 15 cwt utility lorry, liveried as POED, Denman Street, SE1 courtesy of BT Group Archives. Ref: TCB 417/E 7769.

By the 1930s The Post Office Engineering Department comprised of fifteen districts, each in charge of a Superintending Engineer under the control of the Engineer-in-Chief in London.

Mid-Bronze Green

Motor Transport Branch:
The Mechanical Transport Section of POSD (Post Office Stores Department) was transferred to the Engineer-in-Chief to become the Motor Transport Branch of the Engineering Department in a phased transfer between July and October 1931.

The Road Transport Fleet was set up in 1948-1949 to take bulk supplies from manufacturers whose goods (cable, ducting, etc.,) were previously carried by rail. This Road Haulage fleet of the Engineer-in-Chief was merged with the Supplies Department on 1 July 1963. Green vehicles were repainted red following the merger.

Engineer- in-Chief Motor Transport Branch
Under the Engineer-in-Chief, the MTB fleet took the green livery of the established Post Office Engineering Department.

Engineer-in-Chief, GPO, Motor Transport Branch London. Leith House, Gresham Street, EC2.
Photo: Crown copyright (circa 1948). Sourced by POVC.

Styling the Post Office

Post Office Telephones
The 1930s saw the Bridgeman Report (Aug '32) which gave key recommendations about the organisation of the Post Office. The appointment of Sir Stephen Tallents (01/10/33) introduced the first Public Relations Officer (PRO) into the business. These two events strongly influenced how the Post Office both presented and marketed its image.

Thus, within the Post Office Engineering Department from about 1934, POST OFFICE TELEPHONES was used in preference to GPO or POED on the green fleet.

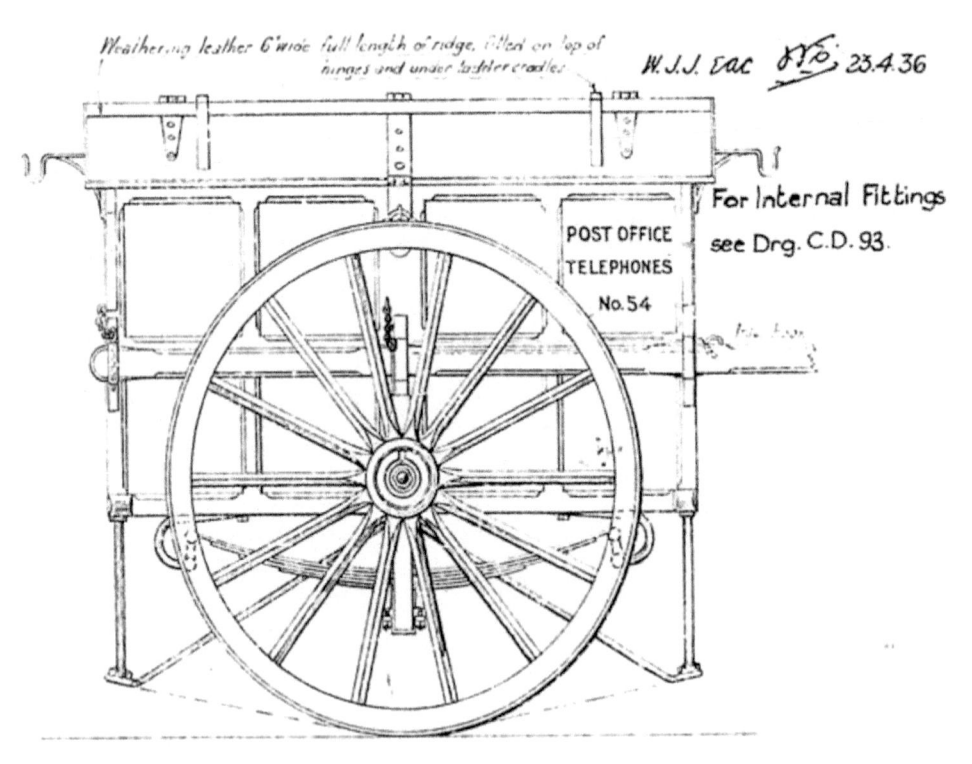

Drawing C.D. 93 of handcart dated 24 April 1936 showing POST OFFICE TELEPHONES. *Source:THGR.*

From about 1934 van chassis ordered from Morris, Morris-Commercial, and Albion were sent on to selected bodybuilders so that the coachwork to GPO designs could be constructed to its requirements.

Mid-Bronze Green

Post Office Telephones, Sectional Engineers Headquarters

Photo: Crown copyright (circa 1934). Sourced by POVC.
Post Office Telephones, Sectional Engineers Headquarters Serial U 6580.

For motor vehicles of the POED, lettering was a bespoke font based upon Gill Sans. The compacted letter O allowed the overall width of the signwriting to be reduced to a manageable proportion. The fitting of long titles onto vehicles continued to be a major consideration for graphic designers throughout the decades.

By the end of March 1936, the GPO fleet (red and green) operated the following numbers of vehicles: Postal services 6204; Engineering services 5030; Telegraph delivery 264; Stores Department transport 57.

Styling the Post Office

Post Office Telephones, Telephone Manager
Departmental re-organisations led circa 1936 to SECTIONAL ENGINEER being replaced by TELEPHONE MANAGER (Area name) on telephone vehicles.

> All inscriptions to be in white block characters.
> On radio investigation vans
>   POST OFFICE
>   RADIO SERVICE
> Will appear instead of
>   POST OFFICE
>   TELEPHONES

Restored Morris Commercial JUW 830 serial U48545 at Amberley Museum © J. Chenery (2011). Lettering extract from Drawing M.T. 81 Lettering for Engineering Vehicles. Post Office Engineering Department: 23.12.36 Engineer-in-Chief's Office. [Image from THGR.]

Mid-Bronze Green
By the mid-1960s these green Morris J2s were commonly seen on subscriber provision and repair duties.

Exceptionally, this J2 example doesn't display the usual POST OFFICE TELEPHONES legend, but it does include the St. Edward's crown.

Above: BMC Morris J2 15cwt utility van 1966 DLL 808C serial U110710 in preservation visiting Amberley Museum © Mark Skillen (2019).

R.M.T.O. (Regional Motor Transport Officer) Camelford House, London. Thought to be from a batch of 1000 vans produced in Jan 1965.

Right: An Aug 1967 registered Morris 30cwt utility van SGW 525F.
Photo (November 1968), courtesy of BT Group Archives. Ref: TCB 417/E 39325.

Gang Morris FG. Long ladders were accommodated through flaps in the upper body section to overhang the cab, which included seating typically for a cabling crew.

Styling the Post Office

Vehicle Signwriting - By 1969 the signwriting of vehicles was specified as:

Area Vehicles

In a Telephone Manager's Area, the standard signwriting for telecommunications vehicles, other than those engaged on radio interference work is:

POST OFFICE TELEPHONES
Telephone Manager
… (Insert T. M.'s headquarters town)

For vehicles on radio interference work, the signwriting is:

POST OFFICE RADIO SERVICE
Telephone Manager
… (Insert T. M.'s headquarters town)

In London, Manchester, West Midland and Scotland West Area, it is necessary to amplify the standard inscriptions to include the name of the Area concerned, e.g.:

POST OFFICE TELEPHONES (or POST OFFICE RADIO SERVICE)
Telephone Manager
Scotland West Area
Glasgow

Regional Vehicles

For Regional headquarters Telecommunications vehicles, other than those engaged on radio interference work, the standard signwriting is:

POST OFFICE TELEPHONES
The Director
… (Insert Region or Country)
… (Insert Director's headquarters town)

Mid-Bronze Green

For Regional headquarters vehicles on radio interference work, the signwriting is:

POST OFFICE RADIO SERVICE
The Director
… (Insert Region or Country)
… (Insert Director's headquarters town)

Telecommunications Headquarters Vehicles

The standard signwriting for Headquarters vehicles is simply:

POST OFFICE TELEPHONES

No names or addresses of Departments, Divisions or Branches should be given.

Supplies Division Vehicles

Vehicles used by the Supplies Division should be signwritten:

POST OFFICE SUPPLIES DIVISION
17/19 Bedford Street
London, W.C. 2

Radio Station Vehicles

For vehicles at radio stations, the signwriting is

P.O. Radio Station
… (Insert name of site)

Extracted from:
P.O. ENGINEERING INSTRUCTION: TOOLS & TRANSPORT
VEHICLES C0015
Issue 5 16.04.69

Styling the Post Office

Yellow for Safety

Explanation…
Engineering Safety July 1968 Issue no.5
"To boost staff and public safety on the roads, the Post Office Telecommunications transport fleet of 40,000 vehicles is to be painted golden yellow. It will be a gradual transformation spread over five years and effected as new vehicles are delivered and old vehicles are dealt with under the normal repainting cycle."

Green meets yellow at Amberley Museum: A Mid-Bronze Green Morris Minivan 167 ELP 5cwt utility, Post Office Telephones -Telephone Manager - East Area – London, serial U88235 © J. Chenery (2011).

The Yellow Fleet
The green fleet was progressively re-liveried in *Golden Yellow* from autumn 1968.
See chapter 9 for the progression to safety yellow.

8: Towards Corporation Status

A booklet was produced explaining the move towards the Post Office becoming a corporation. This included organisational trees of how the business was to be restructured.
Scan from author's collection c1967.

"The Post Office needs to be reconstructed quickly into two separate businesses – Post and Telecommunications because each has widely different operating characteristics and problems."

"The Corporation will take over fully on 1st October 1969."

White Paper
On 3 August 1966, the new Postmaster-General (Edward Short) announced that the Government had decided that the Post Office should become a public corporation. A White Paper (Cmnd. 3233) was subsequently published on 21 March 1967. In November 1966 the PMG told Parliament that the Post Office Savings Department would remain part of the Civil Service and would report to Treasury Ministers. It was to be known in future as the National Savings Department.

'Reorganisation of the Post Office' presented to Parliament by the Postmaster-General by command of Her Majesty, March 1967.
[LONDON HER MAJESTY'S STATIONERY OFFICE PRICE 1s. 9d NET - *TCB 712/1 BT Group Archives.*]

The Corporation will be known as "The Post Office." Her Majesty the Queen has been pleased to approve that the title "Royal Mail" should continue, and that the Corporation should use the Crown and the Royal Cypher as the Post Office does at present. The Sovereign's head will continue to be included in the design of stamps and postal orders. Postage stamp designs will be considered jointly by the Corporation and by the Minister and submitted to Her Majesty by the latter.

Traditionally, the Post Office has followed the organisational pattern of a central Government Department. This pattern is not appropriate for the successful management of a large service industry like the Post Office.

Styling the Post Office

A fundamental examination of the organisation is therefore now being carried out to see what changes are called for to fit it to the future needs of the Post Office, whatever its status. Where appropriate, changes will be implemented in advance of vesting day.

The Post Office makes use of certain services provided by other Government Departments, primarily the Ministry of Public Building and Works and Her Majesty's Stationery Office. This arrangement will continue.

Post Office Act 1969
(1969 c.48, 25th July 1969*) "An Act to abolish the office of master of the Post Office…"*

The Bill to change the status of the Post Office from a government department to a public authority received Royal Assent on 25th July 1969. An Order in Council, made on 31st July 1969, appointed 1st October 1969 as Vesting Day.

Telecom Corporate Colours
At the board meeting held at Post Office Headquarters on 6 December 1967 it was first suggested to adopt green on yellow as the corporate colours for telecommunications as yellow on red had already been chosen for posts. [BT Group Archives TCB 14/10.]

COURIER
The staff newspaper reported: *"On October 1 the new Post Office was born. Courier marks its arrival with this special supplement, recording the historic change-over. Overnight more than 400,000 staff — the country's largest workforce — ceased to be civil servants. The old headquarters at St Martin's-le-Grand near St Paul's becomes the hub of the postal business."*

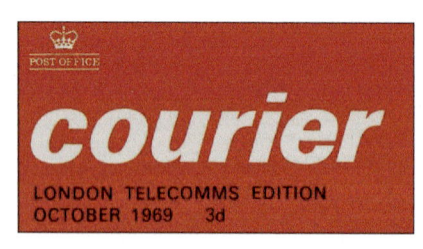

The GPO monogram was replaced by POST OFFICE between two parallel lines.

PHQ as referred to at St. Martin's-le-Grand was originally GPO North. THQ was 2-12 Gresham Street, and Central HQ (CHQ) for board members was at 23 Howland Street near to the Post Office Tower complex.

Towards Corporation Status

The Post Office
Alternative names for the new Post Office corporation were sought by PMG Edward Short in the Jan 1967 edition of Courier. None of the suggested names were favourable, and eventually in June 1968, Prime Minister Harold Wilson confirmed that the organisation would continue as the Post Office.

A corporate identity program for the Post Office corporation

In Aug 1969 Richard Stevens, Design Manager, and Raymond M. Stanley, Head of Publicity Division suggested that 'The Phone Service' might be a suitable name for the telecommunications part of the new Post Office corporation.

Letter to Stuart Rose Design Adviser: On 29 September 1969 the chairman AWC Ryland wrote:

"... [due to a review] the shape of the new Post Office will not emerge for 12 months, and meanwhile it would be premature to consider what our symbol, house style, letter style, and so on should be. ...to continue with the present temporary design, involving two horizontal bars and using the terms Post Office and where necessary, the present accepted name of the business; telecommunications, posts, NDPS and Giro." [NDPS: National Data Processing Service.]

The new monogram (also known as the new crest) devised by Stuart Rose was used throughout the Post Office. The typeface was Clarendon.

Additionally, *Post Office Telecommunications* was used from early 1970 to describe the telephone side of the business.

Cheltenham font was used for *Post Office Telecommunications* until the new Banks and Miles alphabet was ready and authorised.

Design Division wrote a retrospective summary of corporate identity guidelines in 1988. *"The use of the Royal Arms, GPO lozenge [monogram] and the marks composed of the crown surmounting the words Post Office between two horizontal rules, ceased in February 1972."*

Clearly, because of the delay in agreeing new logos, the crown between two horizonal lines had to be retained much longer, in fact up to 1979.

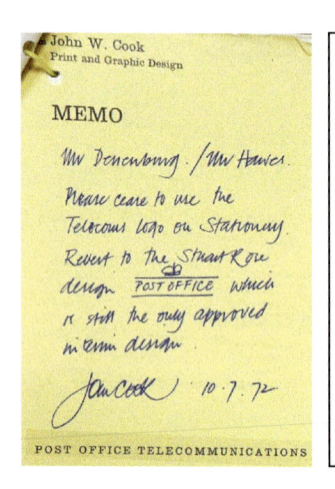

Memo from John Cook (within Post Office Telecommunications) advising to only use the Stuart Rose logo 10/07/1972.

"Mr Denenberg /Mr Hawes. Please cease to use the Telecoms logo on stationery. Revert to the Stuart Rose design which is still the only approved design."

Elsewhere, discussions about use of non-standard HLP (headed letter paper) took place. 12 September 1974 V. W. May TMk3.1.3

"Until there is a comprehensive Corporate Identity design acceptable to MDT [Managing Director Telecoms] and put into effect, it would seem logical to present to the general public, an image of the Business that is not fragmented."

Royal Mail

On the postal side, there were concerns that an extended use of the name *'Royal Mail'* to promote the postal carrier aspect, might mislead or detract from the actual corporation name of *'The Post Office.'* As previously mentioned, the public perception was (or should have been) that the Post Office was both the place at which to post letters, and the firm that operated the whole business. Regardless, it was still called the GPO by many people for decades after Vesting Day (01/10/1969).

MDPC: "The change in title of the Post Office on acquiring Corporation status from that of the General Post Office and the creation of the Corporation itself made a review of the way in which the Post Office presented itself to the public in design terms essential."

MDPC: "...it should be mentioned however that the greater use of the title [Royal Mail] as a trading name has the enthusiastic support of our advertising agents and of our own public relations people." [Undated memos from Managing Director (Posts) Committee.]

MD(P) and MD(T)

The Managing Directors of (P) Posts and (T) Telecoms had to ensure that the new Post Office corporation achieved a co-ordinated new identity.

Towards Corporation Status

Post Office Gazette
During 1969, the long-established weekly staff newsletter, the *Post Office Circular* became the *Post Office Gazette*.

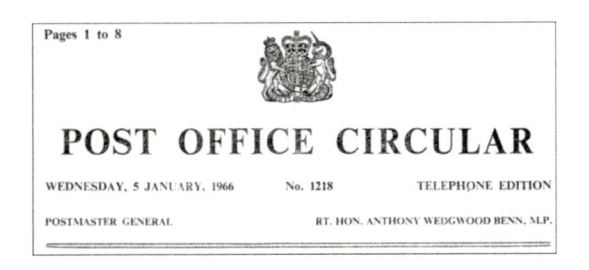

Post Office Circular 5 Jan 1966 Telephone Edition. Post Office Gazette 28 Nov 1979 Complete Edition.

The POST OFFICE monogram continued in use to the end of 1979 by which time Posts and Telecommunications were to get separate identities.
Surprisingly, it wasn't until 1981 that the Post Office as a top level entity began using:

The Post Office as a logotype on its annual reports.

New Designs
It was a step change for the Post Office to even consider how it should present itself to the public.

> Image and style represented the Post Office in the design of its products. The so-called 'modern (plastic) telephone' with dial, (model 706) launched in 1959 was revised to become the 746 in 1967, and the warbling, glow in the dark, Trimphone had been designed in 1964. *Right: A 1/722F 1969 grey/green Trimphone (Author's collection).*

The Trimphone was designed by Martyn Rowlands. However, a different standard style to update the 746 telephone for the modern home was needed.

Styling the Post Office

More Style
In 1969 the Post Office placed a development contract with an industrial designer, David Carter Associates. The *New Style* telephone was produced by the Factories Division (Fac D) and assembled at the Cwmcarn plant in South Wales. The phone was designed to use the dial and transmission circuitry of the long-established (746) *Modern Telephone*. Like fashion, the concept had come full circle because, the phone had a separate bellset, harkening back to pre-1960 ideas. This was to keep the size of the instrument itself small enough to fit on the narrow window ledges of modern homes. Trial versions were tested in Cardiff, Canterbury, and Sheffield Telephone Areas during 1973.

 In 1977 the newly named *Jubilee Compact* version was issued in honour of the Queen's silver accession. In 1978 the *Compact* was added to the telephone rental portfolio, but by this time the market was ready for press-button phones for which the *Compact* could not easily be adapted.

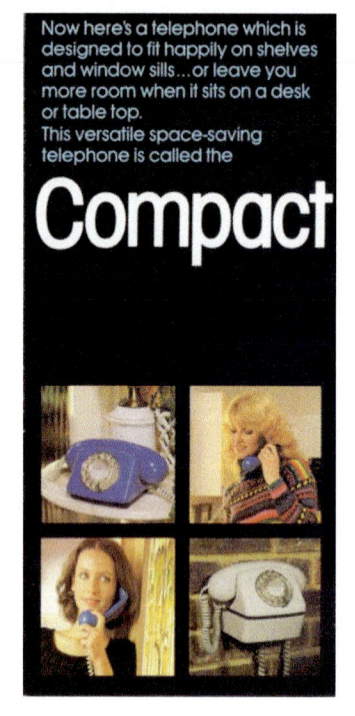

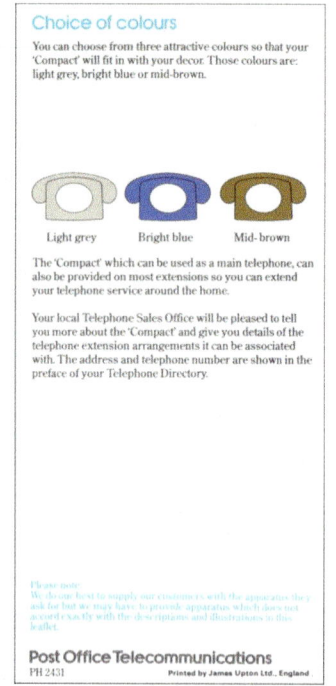

Field trial version of the Compact telephone in light grey. One of the bellset options can be seen top left of the photo.

Tele SA 4271 FWB 72/1
Author's collection.

Leaflet PH 2431: Compact (Tele 776) in Light grey, Bright blue, and Mid-brown.

9: Safety Yellow

British Standard Colour BS381C No. 356 *Golden Yellow*. In preparation for corporation status, and the eventual separation of Posts and Telecommunications, the Post Office Board had finally ratified on 13 May 1968 that green on yellow was to form the identity for the telephone business. This conceptual change towards yellow vans was justified as making them more visible when undertaking cable provision and repair work at the side of the road. Thus, from late 1968 Post Office Telephones began a phased change to a new safety colour of *Golden Yellow* - with light bronze-green lettering, for its fleet of vehicles and trailers. [Reference POST 69/81.]

Restored Post Office Telephones van WLF 801G serial U239358 TELEPHONE MANAGER GUILDFORD visiting Amberley Museum rally © J. Chenery (2010).

Advertising board: 'It's so cheap to phone your friends after six and at weekends.' [Campaign from c1965.]

Styling the Post Office

Telephone Kiosks
It was made clear that the public would not tolerate yellow telephone kiosks, so those would remain red. [Trials of yellow kiosks did take place in the later British Telecom era.]

GPO Registrations
Historically, registrations were issued in blocks by the London County Council (LCC) and later the Greater London Council (GLC) for all new Post Office vehicles, allowing administration from a central point. The GPO registration initially allocated to West Sussex CC was transferred to LCC in 1936 so that the General Post Office could have use of the registration GPO 1 for the latter's new Mobile Post Office (MPO). GPO 2 and 3 were also assigned to MPOs. [The West Sussex local identifiers were BP, PO, and PX between 1903-1974.] GPO registrations allocated were GPO 11-999 (1946), 1-999 GPO (1963), and GPO1-999C (1965). GPO vehicles were re-registered upon resale. PMG was also used as being Postmaster-General. Up to October 1969 Post Office vehicles were operated on 'Her Majesty's Service' and displayed Crown exemption tax discs. Thereafter, licensing of vehicles passed to Head Postmasters and Telephone Managers to apply, as tax was then due as for any normal business fleet.

After gaining corporation status in 1969, Post Office vehicle registrations were issued by

Head Postmasters and Telephone Managers,

not centrally, and

GPO was no longer the initials of the business.

Land Rover 88 (petrol) Station Wagon 1963 Registration 630 GPO TELEPHONE MANAGER CARDIFF © Mike Street (1974).

Safety Yellow

The green lettering was a subtle branding, but the *Golden Yellow* livery was rather more noticeable. The format was POST OFFICE TELEPHONES, TELEPHONE MANAGER, AREA. In 1973 the term GENERAL MANAGER replaced the title TELEPHONE MANAGER and new vehicles were supplied without the Telephone Manager lettering from 1974 with the existing lettering removed after pressure from the General Managers.

Commer van 2500 15cwt utility

POST OFFICE
TELEPHONES
TELEPHONE MANAGER
BLACKBURN

Registration YBV 183M serial 73 314 2180 © Mike Street (1974).

Commer VC
4 ton utility 1972
Registration KFH 440K

GENERAL MANAGER
GLOUCESTER

Photographed at Swindon TEC © Mike Street (1976).

Post Office Telecommunications

The St. Edward's Crown continued to be included on telecommunication vehicles. The new business name of 'Post Office Telecommunications' was in use from early 1970 on printed documents but did not officially appear on vehicles until 1975.

Early use of the wording 'Post Office Telecommunications': Lettering for 'South West Telephones' vehicles 27.11.1972 Drawing 106010 (from THGR).

As was sometimes the case, the Post Office contradicted its own policies when local initiatives pre-empted final authority to implement changes which almost inevitably would take place, albeit with minor alterations. In fairness these may have been field trials, but the company was so large that maintaining adherence on everything was almost impossible, especially during long drawn out transitions!

Henri Henrion

Consultant designer Henri Henrion had promulgated ideas of a radically new Post Office identity as early as 1965, which included using yellow as the primary colour for the telecommunications business. However, his comprehension of the organisation was not appreciated and thus, for the new corporate image, advice was sought from other established companies.

Banks and Miles

Feb 1970: *"To initiate the visual design programme for the Post Office a Design Advisory Committee (DAC) to the Board with Mr Whitney Straight as Chairman has been formed."*

Firms invited to pitch were Banks and Miles, Conran Design Group, Crosby/Fletcher/Forbes, and Design Research Group. In September 1970 Banks and Miles was chosen as most attractive firm, with ideas suitable for further development. Subsequently, within the Post Office, a Graphic Design Unit was established to assist with the implementation of the new corporate identity. Design Director for PHQ (Postal Headquarters), Stuart Rose was also part of the Postal Design Steering Group.

10.1: Banks and Miles

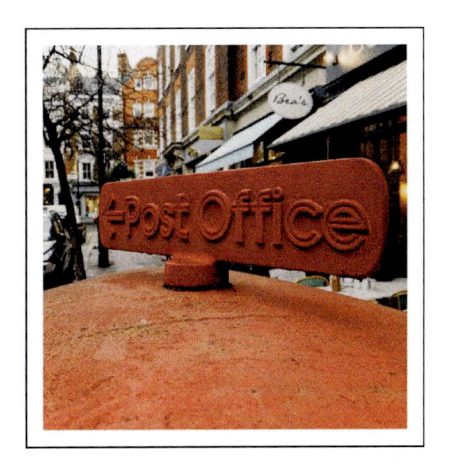

*Above: Scans of Banks and Miles letterheads and stationery.
Left: A Banks and Miles styled Post Office direction sign atop an older London pillar box © Wallace Henning (2017).*

POD Signs (3000-type)
Post Office Direction (POD) signs atop of pillar boxes would point to the nearest post office, usually adjacent. In 1980 a new design of pillar box, the 'Type K' by Tony Gibbs also featured a revised POD. Instead of the traditional oval-shape, the 3000-type sign was rectangular, made of cast aluminium, and featured Banks and Miles' PO Double Line typeface. Originally, yellow type on a red background made them very noticeable.

A Visual Identity Programme for the Post Office
The partnership of Banks and Miles was contracted in 1970 to design a new corporate identity for the Post Office following its change to corporation status in October 1969. An eye-catching lined alphabet was devised that could be used to create a co-ordinated brand across both the telephone and postal businesses. Authority to implement a design programme was initially delayed for 12 months while the new corporation reviewed its operations.

The full story of the Post Office's machinations in deciding the exact details of its new corporate identity runs to hundreds of pages of meetings, memos, letters, and test graphics. Previous associations of operating 'On Her Majesty's Service' together with use of the royal cypher (EIIR) and crown had to be carefully considered. Suggested use of the royal coat of arms may have implied royal appointment, so this idea was not adopted. Chapters 10.1, 10.2, and 10.3 depict the development of ideas that were implemented.

Styling the Post Office

Banks & Miles (1958-1996)

In London 1958, Colin Banks (1932-2002) co-founded Banks & Miles, designers, and typographers, with John Miles. Colin Banks: *"There was no competition in graphic design in the late 1950s, but there was no demand for it either."* John Miles: *"We took up typography because we thought we'd make the world a better place. There was a huge amount of idealism in the early 1950s and Colin was very idealistic indeed."*

Banks and Miles Studio

Above: John Miles and Colin Banks in their London studio circa 1973. A 1970s era design office/studio. Smartly dressed team members. Sturdy desks and chairs. A non-carpeted floor.

Design work/posters set out on noticeboards around the room. The commonplace two-tone colour dial telephones.

Photos this page and opposite: Courtesy of Banks and Miles Archive, Lettering, Printing and Graphic Design collections, Department of Typography & Graphic Communication, University of Reading

Banks and Miles

Banks and Miles Studio

Note the very lofty ceiling with a mix of fluorescent and pendant incandescent lamps. Air con provided by opening windows. Filing cabinets and shelving units serve to divide the working areas and to accommodate all the paperwork. Letters and memos typed on an electric typewriter.

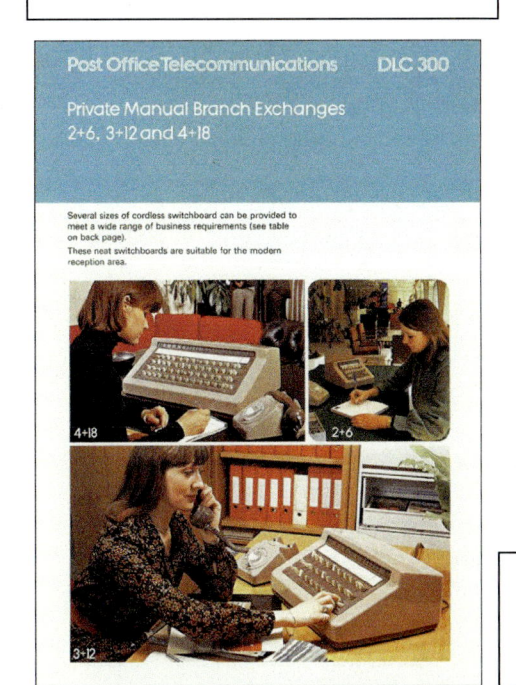

A grey 2 + 6 PMBX (modern switchboard), together with a two-tone grey dial telephone provides two exchanges lines and up to six extensions.

Leaflet DLC 300 (circa 1977) depicts the fully developed 'Post Office Double Line font.' Scan from Telecommunications Heritage Group Resource www.thgr.org.uk

"It was probably the first time an alphabet alone was used to identify an organization."

Styling the Post Office

Pitching the Post Office

A corporate identity scheme for the Post Office by Banks and Miles.
Presented to the Post Office Design Committee 14 July 1970.

Slide opposite: Note the considered spelling of Telecommunications.

```
Post Office
─────────────────────────────────────────
Royal Mail              TeleComunications
Post Brenhinol          Telephones
                        Telex
                        Datel
─────────────────────────────────────────
Giro                    Confravision
National
Data Processing
Service
```

The National Data Processing Service (NDPS) was established in July 1967 to handle the emerging computing needs of the Post Office and Government. In 1977 the service became the DPE (Data Processing Executive).

National Giro: A new banking service was established by the Post Office on 18 October 1968. In 1972 National Giro became a separate business within the Post Office corporation

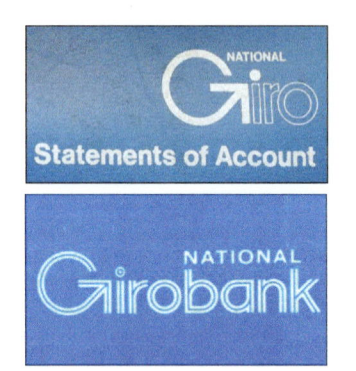

Top: Original Giro lettering. Below: Typeface reworked to Post Office Double Line alphabet but retaining the unique G symbol.

It had been the intention from the outset that Giro should retain blue as its house colour and continue the use of its existing G symbol. Following the introduction of the postal scheme the new lettering could be introduced into Giro. In 1978 National Giro changed its name to National Girobank

And thus began a decade of design work to create, develop and evolve a unified set of identities for the Post Office/Post Office Telephones, Royal Mail, and Girobank. And from 1980 a complimentary, but strikingly different design for the spun-off British Telecom.

John Miles: *"We wanted there to be some continuity with the past which is why Mail vans remained red and Telecommunications vans yellow."*

Post Office Telecommunications

The suggested new name of *TeleComunications* as an identity was discarded, and the full wording *Post Office Telecommunications* began to be used in place of the legacy name, *Post Office Telephones*.

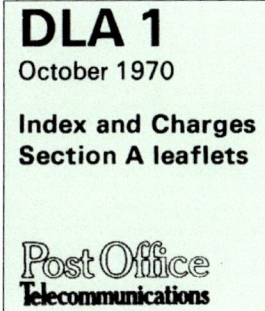

The *Post Office Telecommunications* text uses the Cheltenham styled font because this work pre-dates Banks and Miles' new letterset.

Centre: Descriptive Leaflets (A series) used an interim logo from late 1970. Left: Banks and Miles designed the booklet 'The Post Office Tower London' which was publicity handout PH 1676 12/70 [December 1970]. Scan from author's book collection.

Post Office Double Line

An exercise in letter construction (by John Banks) from January 1969 was developed into a finished alphabet, which was to become the corporate typeface of the Post Office. In 2014 John Banks took a retrospective look back at the work processes involved in producing the new Post Office image, which included the unique double-lined alphabet.

"I just thought it would be fun to do a double-lined alphabet and fiddling with it as a geometric alphabet. I was quite into geometry at the time. We needed to find an alphabet that would be different and characteristic. I said to David Deadman 'I've been fiddling with this alphabet shall I bring it in.' He said: 'Yeah why don't you.' That's how it developed." David was the third designer who worked most consistently on the Post Office scheme. [Banks and Miles quotes are from Matthew Standage's dissertation 2014: *The Post Office corporate identity 1965–1980*.]

The Design Advisory Committee at 23 Howland Street on 26 May 1971 agreed that the new Post Office alphabet should be called POST OFFICE DOUBLE LINE.

Styling the Post Office

Double Line Alphabet

Right: Line out, first draught 10-11 Jan 1969. From: Banks and Miles Archive, Lettering, Printing and Graphic Design collections, Department of Typography & Graphic Communication, University of Reading.

Below: The finished Post Office Typefaces in 1974 [Sheet issue 1/74.] Note the much developed letter b.

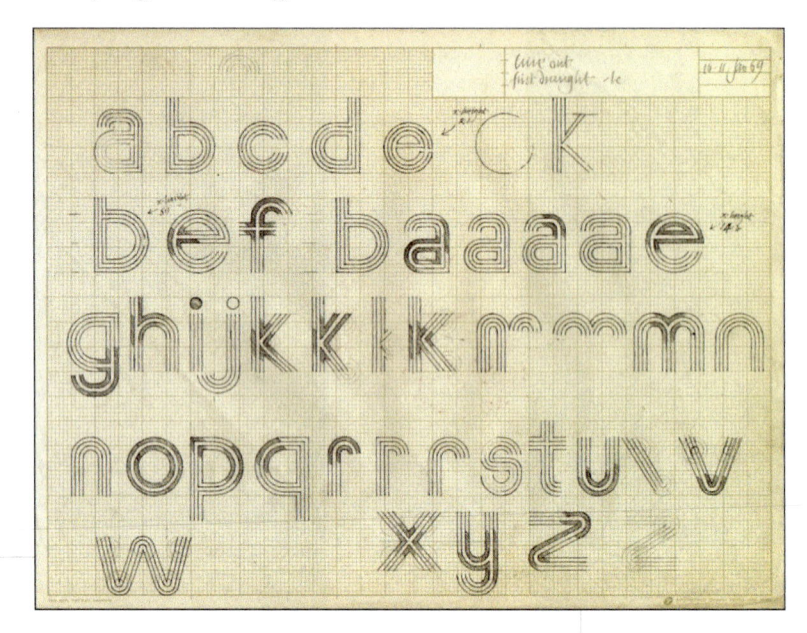

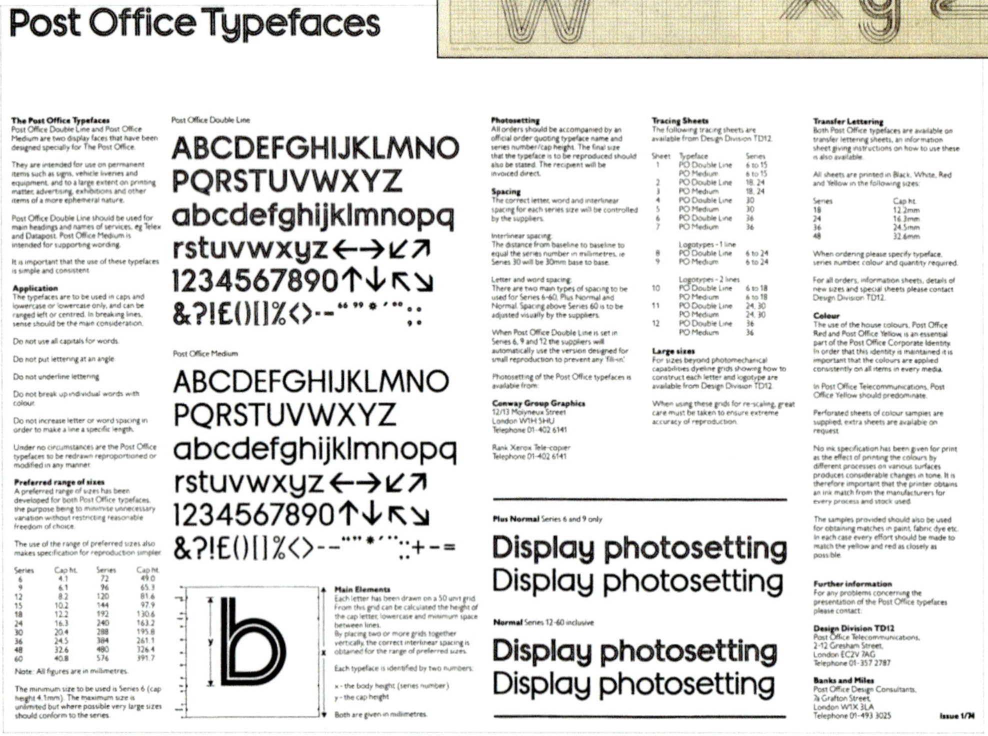

Banks and Miles

John Miles: *"Helvetica seemed to go well with our double line alphabet and, very importantly, it was available in Letraset which was vital for preparing finished dummies and artwork."*

Letraset was a dry-transfer (rubdown) process to apply inked letters onto paper or other materials. The letterset required was (usually) supplied on plastic-backed sheets with an appropriate mix of letters and/or numbers.

Left: Post Office Telecommunications Letraset sheets.
Courtesy of BT Group Archives.
Ref: BT1-COM6/2/1333 Corporate Identity Programme.

Letraset was widely available in stationers throughout the 1970s in the years before word-processors and home computers. Key business names and products were printed in PO Double Line type, with the qualifier using Helvetica, viz:

Electronic post
A Royal Mail Service

Colour {from Post Office Typefaces panel opposite page}
The use of house colours, Post Office Red and Post Office Yellow, is an essential part of the Post Office Corporate Identity. In order that this identity is maintained it is important that the colours are applied consistently on all items in every media. In Post Office Telecommunications, Post Office Yellow should predominate. No ink specification has been given for print as the effect of printing the colours by different processes on various surfaces produced considerable change in tone. It is therefore important that the printer obtains an ink match from the manufacturers for every process and stock used. The samples provided should be used for obtaining matches in paint, fabric dye etc. In each case every effort should be made to match the yellow and red as closely as possible.

Building Signs

Post Office Single Line font was used for the lettering on Baynard House, London (opened 1979). The first production junction tandem System X exchange (TXD14) was BIS (brought into service) here in July 1980.
Left: Baynard House, London © J. Chenery (2010).

The main uses of the Royal Insignia (Jan 1970)

1. Sovereign's Head: On postage stamps and postal orders.
2. Royal Cypher: On pillar boxes, postal vehicles, and certain Post Office buildings.
3. Royal Crown: Used in conjunction with the Cypher and as part of the GPO Crest on Stationery, uniforms, and a wide variety of Post Office property. Also used on its own on, inter alia, telecommunications vehicles and telephone kiosks (up to the K6).
4. Royal Coat of Arms: On the sorting carriages of Travelling Post Offices, on exhibitions devoted to stamps and on stamp presentation packs.

Proposed Van Liveries (July 1970)

Left: Vans showing the intended liveries, both with PO Double-Line lettering. A red Royal Mail van displaying a coat of arms, and a yellow telecommunications van with a T-logo.

Photo is from slide booklet: 'A corporate identity scheme for the Post Office' by Banks and Miles (July 1970).
Ref: POST 154/495.

Photo © Royal Mail Group (2022), courtesy of The Postal Museum.

These van liveries weren't fully adopted. Instead, the Royal Cypher and Crown was used on Royal Mail vans, together with the wording 'Royal Mail.' And just the Crown appeared on telecommunication vans, with the full wording 'Post Office Telecommunications.'

The Design Advisory Committee was concerned that proposals for greater use of the term *'Royal Mail'* to describe the postal service might lead to a dilution of the Post Office brand, especially if post office counters ever dropped the name Post Office. History shows that the Royal Mail brand did eventually dominate, many decades later, leaving *Post Office Counters* as the only remaining portion of the government business that was once the all-encompassing General Post Office.

10.2: Banks and Miles Postal

Left: Leyland Roadrunner, Besco Mailvan C373 YNF serial 5190288 (1985) © Mike Street (1986).
Right: Morris Marina Mailvan OCU 199X serial 2060471 (1982) © Mike Street (1987).

It took until December 1974 to finally agree the details for postal liveries. Banks and Miles' scheme was then gradually introduced from January 1975 onwards.
Any further changes of liveries wouldn't be so much of a problem as in earlier years because, from September 1971 vinyl transfers had been used for new vehicle deliveries, allowing designs to be removed and replaced at local motor transport workshops.

Post Office Gazette *[Subpostmasters' Edition 8 Dec 1982]*

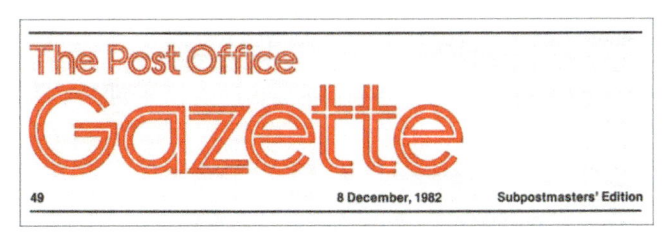

The Post Office Gazette was printed in several different issues, such as Complete Edition, Subpostmasters' Edition, and others. With the later split of businesses, the Telephone Edition became the Telecom Gazette.

Styling the Post Office

The Post Office Design Guidelines {April 1988 from POST 154/555}
[By this period, the telecommunications functions were no longer part of the Post Office]

Barry Robinson, Design Adviser for the Post Office:
One design guide for the Corporation, Letters, Parcels and Counters and the elements they share. This lettering is a 'display' typeface that has been specially designed to link together visually all parts of the business. It is under copyright for exclusive use by The Post Office.

The Post Office

{Corporate Administration} Chairman's Office, Secretary, Solicitors, Board Members, Public Relations.
{General Administration} Post Office Headquarters, Regional Post Office Headquarters, Head Post Offices (Executive function).
For use on Stationery, Publicity, Forms.

Royal Mail

{Services} Royal Mail: Mail services, Publicity, Uniforms for postmen, Signs (buildings with no counter services). (Not for use on stationery or forms.)

Post Office

{Services} Public offices Fascia sign for public offices and Sub-Post Offices only.

{Services} Exclusive use as identity for public offices with counter services only.

Typically, Letters, Parcels, and Counters businesses were to be qualified with

'A division of The Post Office Corporation.' 'It is vitally important that the image they promote is seen to be clearly linked to the overall corporation.' [Barry Robinson Design Adviser 21/4/88.]

These sub-businesses went on to develop their own identities, e.g., *Parcelforce*. {See chapter *Royal Mail '90.*}

Colours
The Royal Mail 'red and yellow' identity was expressed as Double Line lettering in yellow being reversed out of a red background. Paints colours in the 1988 Design Guidelines were confirmed as BS 381C Red 539 and Yellow 356.

Special Service Brands
Back in the late 1970s, Royal Mail special service brands highlighted the varying levels of express post, tailored to meet specific customer needs.

Expresspost
A Royal Mail Special Service

Intelpost
A Royal Mail Special Service

Datapost
A Royal Mail Special Service

Swiftair
A Royal Mail Service

Above: Bedford HA mailvan UBO 876S showing the dual Welsh/English lettering Post Brenhinol and Royal Mail in Expresspost livery, Cardiff. Phone: Cardiff 31313. Photo © Mike Street (1978).

Intelpost by fax, Datapost and Expresspost by van and motorbike, and Swiftair by plane. British Telecom launched its own worldwide fax re-transmission service, *Bureaufax* in November 1980. The main Bureaufax office was at Cardinal House, London.

Circa 1977, Expresspost offered a two-hour delivery target within Central London. It also provided same day delivery between major cities.

Datapost 1970

Datapost was a same day delivery service targeted at companies who needed to send data, in the form of tapes/discs/computer printouts across the UK. High-speed data transfer by private wires or landlines was restrictive by cost and technical capacity when the service was first established.

Left: A 1982 Freight Rover Sherpa K2 1.8D 240cf High-roof Mailvan registration A568 AWV © Mike Street. Below: A Datapost/Sameday Kawasaki motorcycle © J. Chenery (2012).

Left: A 1976 Commer Mailvan PNG 751R serial 6090118 at Lowestoft © Mike Street (1977).

Commer vans had been used since the mid-1960s by the Post Office; the Dodge Spacevan (next page) was the last incarnation to operate with Post Office Telecommunications/ British Telecom. The majority rusted away, so any in preservation are rare.

Only postal transport used the Royal Cypher (EIIR) and Crown. Telecom vehicles used the Crown only.

10.3: Banks and Miles Telecommunications

Left: Post Office Telecommunications Dodge 15cwt Spacevan XYL 71T in store at Museum of London © J. Chenery (2009).
Below: Crown with door lettering.

Note that the transfers were applied with a slightly incorrect spacing during restoration!

Post Office Telecommunications

"This vehicle was purchased from Chrysler UK Ltd. and went into service on 17 August 1978. Operating around Rushey Green in the British Telecom London South East Area, it worked on external maintenance as fleet no. 78 314 0678."

By 1975 the visual identity of Post Office Telecommunications had finally been agreed.

Telecommunications Instruction
K MANAGEMENT GENERAL 4 Organisation D0010 Issue 1 Oct 1975:

VISUAL IDENTITY: POST OFFICE TELECOMMUNICATIONS
The Business is to be identified formally by the name Post Office Telecommunications in full. It will not be abbreviated. For display purposes the name Post Office Telecommunications should be in Post Office In Line letters with an alternative in Post Office Medium alphabet in the smaller sizes. Post Office alphabets should not be used for text. The crown is to be used on vehicles and telephone directories.

Styling the Post Office

Post Office Supplies Division

The Post Office Supplies Department was allocated to the telecommunications business in the Wedgwood-Benn reorganisation of 1968. At the same time, it became part of the Purchasing and Supplies Department with its red vehicles repainted yellow and lettered Supplies Division from autumn 1968.

Post Office Supplies Division,
17-19 Bedford Street, London, WC2E 9HR.

A 1979 Seddon Atkinson motive unit registration DYN 107V painted in Golden Yellow livery with Banks and Miles Double-line red lettering. Photo courtesy of The Post Office.

The Supplies Dept. HQ at 17-19 Bedford Street was designed for the Post Office by the Office of Works and constructed by Higgs & Hill (contractors) between 1883/4. It was a west central district post and telegraph office; the public post office function ceased in 1963.
[british-history.ac.uk/survey-london/vol36/pp253-263#p45]

Regional Variations

As an alternative to the generic **Post Office Telecommunications**, Regions were allowed to display their given names, in this example:
South West Telecommunications with Gloucester Telephone Area, on the door.

Bedford HA utility van ADF 739T serial 78 302 5560 in Marlborough © Mike Street (1978).

London Telephones leaflet: Join the headset (c1980).

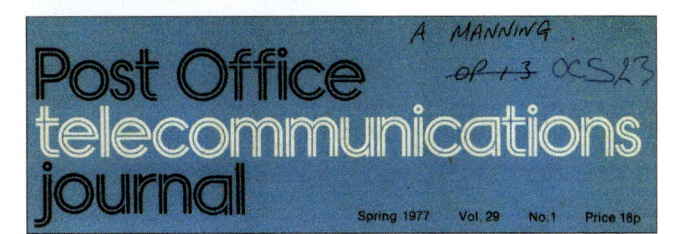

PO Double Line in Use

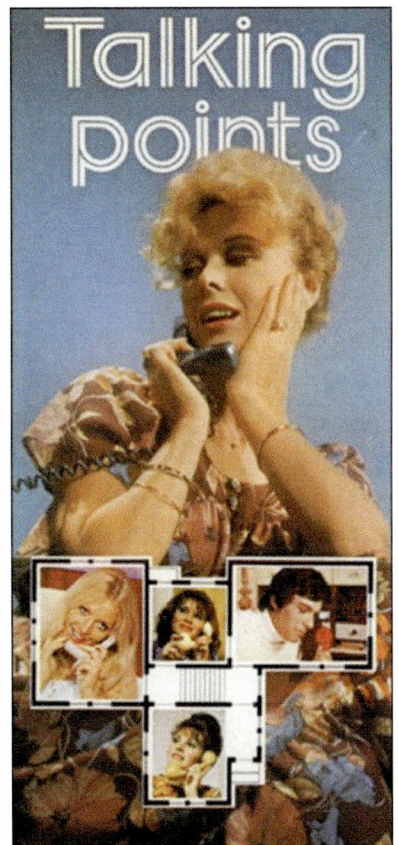

Talking Points telephone marketing leaflet (PH series) 1975 [Scan: Simon Chappell.] SIGNAL March 1976; Maintenance News (8) Autumn 1975; Database the journal of the Post Office Data Processing Service (June 1975). PH (publicity handouts) leaflets PH 2223 11.77 and PH 1950 (9/75).

Styling the Post Office

Telephone Bills
The characteristic letter b of the PO Double Line type was particularly noticeable on telephone bills.

Call Stimulation
The automation of Subscriber Trunk Dialling STD) was progressively introduced from 1958, allowing cheaper self-dialled calls at given times. And thus, the wording (c1965) *'With STD, it's so cheap to phone your friends, after six and at weekends,'* became a catchy advertising slogan.

Buzby
From mid-1976 advertising boards and stickers on the telecom fleet furthered the campaign and popularised the exploits of a little, yellow-feathered bird with the slogan *'Make someone happy with a phone call.'* The subsequent campaigns spawned an inordinate amount of carrier bags, coasters, toys, and merchandising until Buzby (with the voice of Bernard Cribbins) commanded a long-lasting love/hate relationship with the public, which continued into the 1980s.

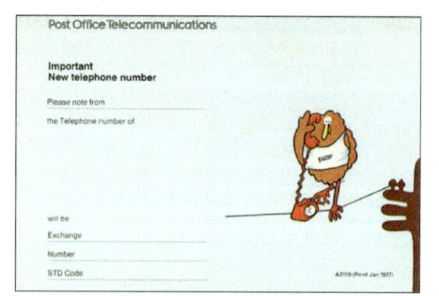

Scans from author's collection.
Van poster: 'A local call goes a long way' courtesy BT Group Archives. Ref: TCC351/THQ 5167 (May 1977).

11: British Telecom

A 1978 British Telecom Bedford CF340 chassis-cab OBV 579T serial 78 327 0026 with lift-off body (Coachwork Conversions) © Mike Street (1981).

British Telecom, London South

Prestel

In the mid-1970s Post Office Telecommunications' viewdata (interactive teletext) dial-up service needed a name that could be trademarked. Brand name consultants Novamark, and Pentagram design consultancy were commissioned to assist. Alex Reid, coined the term *PRESTEL*. *TEL* meaning 'at a distance,' and *PRES* being a prefix that could make a marketable word. The seven letters of the *PRESTEL* name corresponded to the colours on the screen which were green, red, cyan, blue, white, magenta, and yellow. The logo is attributed to Mervyn Kurslanksy. A BT colleague observed, *"In my dad's London office they even had the Prestel logo on the carpets!"* [This was probably in Lutyens House which was Prestel's London head office.] Novamark, launched by John Matthew Murphy in 1974 was a new British company that went on to become Interbrand, and was sold to Omnicom in 1993. Viewdata was devised by Sam Fedida at the Post Office Research Centre at Martlesham Heath.

British Telecom
Despite the simplicity of well-known names, the complete brand package is often the amalgam of several specialist companies' efforts. Novamark named British Telecom, but the design of the brand (as with the Post Office) was put out to competition and won again by Banks and Miles.

Styling the Post Office

Extracts from British Telecom Design Guidelines [June 1981 folder BT Group Archives.]

Banks and Miles: *"We kept the existing and satisfactory Telecommunications yellow, to give some continuity with the past and because it was a colour so well established that to change it would be unnecessarily expensive. The second colour, blue, works well with yellow and stands out clearly on a light background."*

Colours:

"British Telecom will maintain the existing Telecommunications yellow (BS 5252 No. 08 E 51) as it is an important international safety colour for vehicles which often have to be parked by the roadway.

For the second colour, a bright blue (BS 5252 No. 20 E 56) has been chosen for its contrast with the yellow as well as to provide a good background for black or white."

The two Telecom colours should always be used on permanent items, such as vehicles and signs although for more ephemeral items such as publicity or advertising a range of compatible colours may also be used.

British Telecom Yellow	**British Telecom Blue**
BS 5252 No. 08 E 51	BS 5252 No. 20 E 56
Pantone 123	Pantone 300

BS 5252 became a standard in 1976 with the aim of extending the range of the older BS 2660.
[Author's note: Pantone 123 equates to BS 381C 356 Golden Yellow.]

Logotype, symbol, dot/dash strip
'The design elements of the British Telecom Visual Identity consist of the logotype, symbol, dot/dash strip, British Telecom colours, yellow and blue, and supporting Helvetica typeface.'

British Telecom

Banks and Miles: *"It had to have an ingredient that would make the break from the Post Office appear clean and unequivocal."*

Dot/dash…for when and additional decorative element is needed to give 'attack' to the visual identity in the marketplace. When used as an extension of the logotype the minimum number of dots and dashes to be used are **five** dots and **four** dashes. …it always starts and finishes with a dot.

British Telecom – part of the Post Office
The British Telecom identity was announced to staff, (via pre-printed Board memos) on 20 May 1980. *"The style chosen is based upon a version of the trading name TELECOM. We will retain the basic house colour of yellow, but all lettering will be blue instead of red."* Kenneth F. Leeson, Chairman, Eastern Telecommunications Board.

British Telecom's new identity gradually moved away from the Post Office and was finally privatised in 1984. During the transition which started in June 1980, British Telecom was shown as being 'part of the Post Office.'

Scan of leaflet PH 2492 (1/81).

From June 1980 until demerger in October 1981, effectively the telecommunications business of the Post Office was trading as British Telecom. From floatation in 1984, the privatised company British Telecommunications plc was then trading as British Telecom.

Letraset

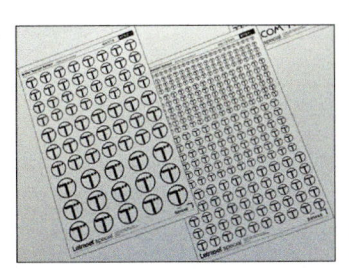

Helvetica, the supporting typeface, and Letraset transfers continued to be used to create the telecom identity.

British Telecom Fleet

Left: A longer dot/dash identity was applied to larger vehicles early in the branding scheme.

Bedford TK truck CVF 583T East Anglia District Norwich © David Cott.

Right: A restored 1980s British Telecom Bedford HA 110 GHM 578W serial 803028623 badged London North West visiting Milton Keynes Museum © J. Chenery (2015).

Post Office/BT ladders were always notable for having three sections.

The fleet of *safety yellow* vans was retained, and the blue lettering was a striking contrast to the previous red double line typeface identity of Post Office Telecommunications. In later decades, rear end chevrons, reflective vinyls, and strict roadworks guarding, somewhat negated the need for such bright paintwork on vehicles engaged in or parked during work along the roadside.

The Author's K8

In 1968 as the new K8 kiosk was about to be introduced, the GPO was considering adopting yellow as its house colour for telecommunications. The implications of having bright yellow telephone kiosks in London, where red boxes were sacrosanct was almost too much to contemplate!

In Jan 1980, *Telecom Today* reported:
"As an experiment, more than 80 kiosks in the north-west [Greater Manchester and Liverpool] have been painted in a special long-lasting paint in bright British Telecom yellow. The casings for the telephone equipment have been treated with black long-lasting paint. We feel that for anyone trying to find a telephone in a hurry, yellow stands out."

This idea was not adopted. Cast iron kiosks remained red. The later KX 100 + series of payphone housings retained elements of red as a nod to the heritage.

Left: This K8 has the earlier Mark 1 roof. Below: Later castings (1976 onwards) had a modified design to prevent cracking during manufacture.

Left: The author's kiosk resplendent in Golden Yellow © J. Chenery (2019).

Styling the Post Office

Publications
One of the consequences of privatisation was that British Telecom now had to pay for all its postage charges in full; previously these had been shared/subsidised across the Post Office. Staff magazines which were once posted externally to homes were now distributed internally at the workplace. Mailings of telephone bills and customer correspondence in an era before electronic communications (Internet/e-mail) were considerable.

Below: British Telecom Journal Spring 1980 Volume 1 Number 1 price 24p D. A. Riches MS 1.4.3 [Thanks Duncan!]

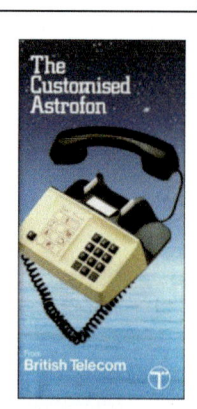

Leaflets: Dawn PHME 2 (4/81); Genie CP/MS3 (8/83); The Customised Astrofon PHME 31 (2/82)
The Telephone Edition of the *Post Office Gazette* became the *Telecom Gazette*.

British Telecom

Plugs, Sockets, and Telephones (PST)

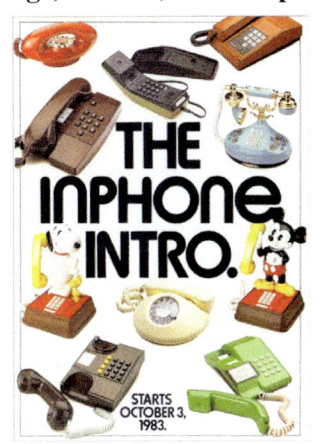

From late 1981 onwards, the Plug, Socket, Telephone (PST) concept allowed customers to have the new standard (white), main and extension sockets fitted to allow portability of wired phones from room to room. (Cordless/wireless phones were only just being developed.) This scheme was in preparation for the liberalisation of the telephone market. And from 1 Jan 1985 British Telecom lost its prime instrument monopoly, which meant that the once mandatory rental and maintenance (a long established revenue stream) of the main telephone was to be swept away. The marketing of a new range of telephones was now more important than ever. Customers needed to be…

Intouch Intone Inphone

Colin Wise (CP's Advertising and Promotions manager) wrote: *"There's never been such high-quality support available before, and it's all an invaluable aid in the selling effort."*

Left: Inphone Insight magazine No.5 November 1985 produced for Consumer Products Division of British Telecom Enterprises.

Inphone 40 second TV ad

All ITV Areas Oct 1983 to March 1984.
MUSIC UP (to the tune of *In Crowd*)
SUNG: I'm in with the *Inphone*. I go…where the *Inphone* goes.
Plug in with the *Inphone*, suits my style, suits my clothes.
Doesn't matter where or what I do…
it's just my new way of getting through.
Inphone's in tone…in touch with me,
Inphone's in tone, in touch with you.
In touch, in tone, *Inphone*.
MVO: *Inphone* from British Telecom. To get yours call 100 and ask for Freefone *Inphone* (music fades).

In Crowd was a 1964 song first performed by Dobie Gray. The MVO in the TV ad was DJ, Mike Read.

Styling the Post Office

KX Kiosks

DCA (David Carter Associates)

In 1960 David Carter CBE RDI founded David Carter Associates (DCA) as *"a multidisciplinary consultancy involved in designing products for mass production."* In 1972 DCA had designed the *Compact* telephone for Post Office Telecommunications. Subsequently, the KX series of kiosks were designed by DCA in 1985 for British Telecom and manufactured by GKN engineering.

Within the new series of kiosks KX100-400, launched by British Telecom in 1985, the KX300 was a triangular shaped enclosure. The range was manufactured by GKN (Guest, Keen and Nettlefolds) engineering.

Photo courtesy of Andrew Emmerson: The KX300 with yellow T-logo and lettering. The engineer's van is an Austin Maestro 500 City, registration E157 FAR.

Business Systems

From about 1985, Business Systems, a division within British Telecom, had its own branding of vans liveried in *Nightwatch Blue* with yellow lettering. Some vans retained the dot/dash telecom lettering.

Photo: Business Systems Ford Fiesta (Popular) G881 HOA © David Cott.

12.1: Post Office Railway

The Post Office Railway (London) opened in 1927 to carry mailbags between Paddington overground station and the Eastern District (letter) Office at Whitechapel, London.

Intermediate stops were notably King Edward Building (Chief Office) and Mount Pleasant sorting and maintenance depot. In essence, it linked sorting offices in London and connected with mainline railway stations.

Static exhibit of Mail Rail unit(s) at Amberley Museum © J. Chenery (2008).

A train consisted of top and tail motive units, plus a low, flat carriage in the middle upon which four mail containers were held. Each container (full of mailbags) had a quick release lever, and could be easily wheeled off the train, level with the platform.

Conveyor belts and chutes carried individual mail bags to and from the platforms and sorting offices above. The manual handling of mailbags between containers was labour intensive.

Operating within the London Postal Region (LPR), the Post Office Railway was an important link in the transporting of mail-by-rail across Great Britain. With trains originally finished in the utilitarian colour of Engineering Green/Mid-Bronze Green, the equipment was in keeping with the colours used by the Post Office Engineering Department. The mailbag container/trolleys were plain metal grey/fabric finish. The railway wasn't a secret, but it wasn't widely known to the public either, so branding was low-key, or non-existent. As the trains ran underground on a closed circuit, only the workers and invited guests viewed their movements.

Royal Mail Letters
With the creation of the business unit *Royal Mail Letters* in October 1986, there was an incentive to assert the *Royal Mail* brand across the company. Travelling Post Offices (TPOs) gained the wording *Royal Mail Letters*. And in 1987 as the Post Office Railway achieved 60 years of running, it was renamed *Mail Rail*. Liveries were red, with *Banks and Mile*s double-line lettering.

Photo: Mail Rail unit, 'The London Flyer' at Mount Pleasant depot © Jason Cross (1991).

Post Office Railway

The London Flyer
Publicity for the rebranded *Mail Rail* included the refitting of three trains (502, 514, 532 of Greenbat manufacture) with fibreglass cowlings which gave the units a very smart appearance. The cowlings on these refurbished trains also slowed the ingress of dust into the traction motors, but no further units were modified in this way. Nameplates used were City of London, Capital Express, and London Flyer. Later names used were Great East Express, and Great West Express.

In 1987 the rest of the *Mail Rail* running stock was repainted in Postal Service Red (No.539).

Left: *A static exhibit of a Mail Rail unit at The Postal Museum, Mount Pleasant © J. Chenery (2018).*

Below: *Dodge Spacevan JWC 968V serial 9540005 at Colchester DO © Brian Forode. Note 'Postal Engineering' in Clarendon font.*

The establishment of Postal Engineering c1968/9 allowed technicians in the Post Office a choice of working for the postal or telecom side of the business.

Postal Engineering included letter sorting machines and signalling equipment on the Post Office Railway.

Styling the Post Office

Postal Engineering
Extract from memo: *Design Identification of the Postal Business MDPC (74) 40.*

1974: That engineering vans should continue to carry the wording "Postal Engineering" and not, as proposed, "Royal Mail Engineering Services."

Expresspost

Circa 1977, *Expresspost* offered a two-hour delivery target within Central London. It also provided same day delivery between major cities. Like *Datapost*, it used courier motorcycles and dedicated carriage slots on *Mail Rail* to achieve its deadlines.

Expresspost leaflet scan from The Postal Museum.

Royal Mail 1990

In 1990 Royal Mail's refreshed branding moved away from the Banks and Miles' corporate style and adopted Stempel Garamond Italic as the primary typeface.

Mail Rail signage and lettering on rolling stock was updated accordingly.

Image: Sample Stempel Garamond Italic.

Mail Rail 1990

Stempel Garamond lettering: Mail Rail tunnel station sign © J. Chenery (2017).

The 1990 rebranding retained the Banks and Miles yellow lettering of Royal Mail in what was known as the Cruciform symbol. White Stempel Garamond Italic font was used for all other lettering.

Mail Rail rolling stock at Debden store © J. Chenery (2014).

End of the Line

The Post Office Railway, *Mail Rail* closed to working traffic in 2003 as Royal Mail reviewed its rail strategy. Modern-day sorting methods (of high volume) had displaced the smaller sorting offices away from the *Mail Rail* interchanges. For such a specialist railway, *Mail Rail* had become outmoded in terms of manual handling of mail, and the extra effort required to operate an aging railway.

On the overground rail network, the last Travelling Post Office (TPO) service ran on the night of 9 January 2004. Hand-sorting of mail on TPOs was labour intensive, and in modern times was perceived as well as being more of a health and safety issue, as trains travelled up to maximum speeds to maintain schedules and routes between increasing passenger and freight traffic.

Styling the Post Office

Mail Rail (2017)
Mail Rail had become a bygone curiosity, and thus it was ideally suited to be re-opened (in part) as a tourist attraction, and to be incorporated into the new Postal Museum at the Mount Pleasant workshop terminus. *Mail Rail* the ride, opened on 28 July 2017.

Above: Warning notice using Banks and Miles double-line type.

Right/Above right: The *Mail Rail* ride attraction features red and green carriages as a nod to previous Post Office Railway rolling stock colours.

Photos © J. Chenery (2017).

The new *Mail Rail* battery trains were created by Severn Lamb, specialists of urban, leisure and resort transport. *Mail Rail* at *The Postal Museum* is operated by the Postal Heritage Trust (charity) and supported by Royal Mail and the Post Office.

12.2: Mail by Rail

Travelling Post Offices (TPOs) for the conveyance, sorting, and transfer of Royal Mail's post on the railways officially date back to the 1838 act of Parliament.

The Railways (Conveyance of Mails) Act 1838 allowed the Postmaster-General to require any railway given notice, to transport mail on behalf of the Post Office.

"...provision should be made by law for the conveyance of the mails by railways at a reasonable rate of charge."

And to dictate, if deemed necessary, that special carriages be fitted out and used.

"...on all carriages for the service of the Post Office there shall be on the outside painted the royal arms, in lieu of the name of the owner, and the number of the carriage."

It is assumed that the colour scheme of postal coaches was always red, but in many instances the railway companies own liveries prevailed, presumably by mutual agreement with the Post Office.

In the post-privatisation years, choices of rolling stock and operational conditions were stipulated in business contracts.

Post Office Sorter coach NSA 80337 at Nene Valley Railway © J. Chenery (2009). Note the markings include the operating company English Welsh & Scottish Railway (EWS).

Styling the Post Office

Mail by Rail
Over the decades, letters, packets, and parcels for the Post Office were conveyed by a variety of high- priority means, forming a joined-up postal system across the UK railway network. This comprised: TPOs, the Post Office Railway, Rail Express Systems (Res), and Railnet.

Travelling Post Offices (TPOs)
The Post Office had a TPO Section within London Postal Region (LPR) that looked after most services (including those away from London).

A Southern Railway malachite green liveried Royal Mail TPO (George VI reign) at Nene Valley Railway © J. Chenery (2009).

The Post Office's brand name *Royal Mail* was used across the overground rail network, but the lesser-known in-house underground scheme, the *Post Office Railway* was quite unobtrusive.

Mail by Rail

Up to the end of 1947 the GB rail network (and trains) was operated and owned by the Big Four (rail) companies: Great Western Railway (GWR); London, Midland and Scottish (LMS); London and North-Eastern Railway (LNER); Southern Railway (SR).

The Great Train Robbery (1963)

What became known as *The Great Train Robbery (GTR)* was not good publicity for either the Post Office/Royal Mail, or the government.

On the night of 7 August 1963, the TPO *Up Special* mail train was carrying letters and HVPs (High Value Packets of bank notes) from Glasgow to Euston. Strangely, the more secure coaches were all out of service. The preceding Scottish Bank Holiday (5 August) meant the total of bank notes was much higher than usual.

In the early hours of 8 August, as the train approached Sears crossing (near Cheddington) it was stopped by a false red signal. The loco and two front carriages were moved to Bridego railway bridge, and a haul of £2,595,997.10s.0d. was unloaded by the robbers.

The mail train was a London, Midland and Scottish (LMS) railway set of 12 TPO coaches in maroon paintwork with gold *Royal Mail* lettering.

Left: GTR exhibition at The Postal Museum
© J. Chenery (2019).

Styling the Post Office

In Models

Tri-ang Hornby model railway stock item R 402. Coach M 30224.

Cost in June 1967 was 26/2 (£1.31 in decimal money).

Photo: Author's collection © (2021).

This Tri-ang Hornby OO-gauge set from the 1960s depicts the Royal Mail name and cypher on the maroon LMS mail coach of the type operated in 1963. This example is coach M 30224. For sake of inclusion the real GTR line up was: Loco D 326 and non-passenger coaching stock (train order) M31016M, 30204, 30289, 30235, 30220, 30277, 30214, 30210, 30275, 30272, 30247 and 30276. M30204M contained the HVPs of returning bank notes, which were the main target of the raid.

High Value Packets – A Post Office Service

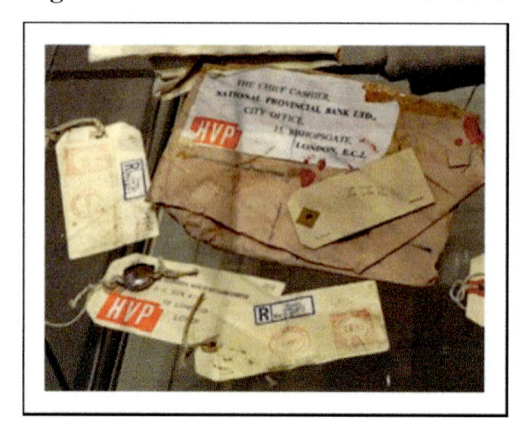

Was a special postal service, only available to banks, which allowed the transfer/exchange between branches of (mostly) used banknotes which were destined for destruction. The *HVP* service operated from 1930 to about 1975. It was replaced by the *Bankers Special Packet* (BSP) which then used private security firms.

Left: HVP exhibits at the GTR exhibition at the Postal Museum © J. Chenery (2019).

Mail by Rail

British Railways
British Railways, part of the British Transport Commission, began on 1 January 1948 and from 1965 traded as British Rail (BR). The final part of BR was privatised on 20 November 1997.

Gangwayed coaches for British Railways were initially red and cream (*Crimson Lake* and Cream); the popular alternative description became *blood and custard*. From 1956 a darker maroon, like the old LMS livery was introduced. Regional variations of liveries gave a less than uniform image for British Railways, but it is not the intention here to track too much BR history. A standardised design of British Railways Mark I coaches was produced between 1951 to 1974. TPOs to LMS design continued to be built until 1958, but from 1959 a total of 145 Mark I TPOs were constructed or adapted from passenger coaches, the last in 1977. BR designed TPOs exceptionally had central, instead of offset, end gangway connections. They were initially finished in Post Office Red, and from 1965 in a variation of British Rail's standard blue and grey. Across BR, it wasn't until 1974 that the last maroon Mark 1 coach was repainted into the blue and grey livery.

Post Office Sorter (POS) W 80301

A Mark 1 type British Rail Post Office Sorting (POS) van no. W 80301 at Great Central Railway © K P Simpson (2010).

Styling the Post Office

Post Office Sorter (POS) NSX W 80301 was built at Wolverton works in 1959. Excepting regional variations, this was the distinctive brand image of Royal Mail TPOs.

Andrew Emmerson remarks: *"This is an example of a hand-drawn (type) design that was supplied (by the Post Office) to transfer manufacturers (almost certainly Tearne & Sons)."*

In the aftermath of the Great Train Robbery (1963), the security of mail on trains was questioned. Revised specifications for extra locks, smaller windows and changes in operating procedures were all considered. Perhaps the instantly recognisable Post Office Red for mail trains had made them an enticing target? This was soon to change!

Johnston and Gill Sans
In 1913 London Underground's (LU's) publicity manager Frank Pick commissioned typographer Edward Johnston to design a company typeface. Pick wanted a corporate style that could be used for LU's informational posters which promoted the Tube. The resulting *Johnston* type was to become an iconic part of Tube travel. William Teasdale, assistant GM of the London and North Eastern Railway (LNER) was enamoured of Frank Pick's choices of stylish poster advertising. Thus, it was logical that Cecil Dandridge (Teasdale's successor) continued a policy of following the leading trend of LU.
Meanwhile, in 1926 Eric Gill inspired by Johnston's typeface, created Gill Sans. Subsequently in 1929 Dandridge commissioned Gill Sans for LNER's own poster and publicity material. Soon after Nationalisation in 1948, British Railways adopted Gill Sans as its official typeface.

British Rail
In 1964 the Design Research Group (DRU) was commissioned to create a unified corporate identity for the newly named British Rail.
Jock Kinneir and Margaret Calvert had earlier produced *Transport*- a sans serif typeface, and it is this that was adapted to form the basis for the *Rail Alphabet* which was soon to be an integral part of British Rail's corporate image.

"January 1965 marks the start of an entirely new look for British Railways. All parts of the system will be given a recognizable house style. The main elements are a new symbol, new livery, and new letter styles." [British Rail poster quote 1964.]

BR Blue and Grey

The new blue and grey livery of British Rail was noticeably used on its Mark II coaches (built between 1964-1975) and was also applied to Travelling Post Offices.

"Blue and grey and blue liveries started to appear in 1965, but workshops had to update their equipment, and blue and grey only started to appear from all workshops in 1966."

M80342 NSX at Stafford 28/04/1987 showing the red posting box panel © Steve Jones. NSX is a TOPS code: Post Office Sorting Van - Dual air and vacuum braked.

Rail Blue to BS 381C No. 114
Grey to BS 2660 No. 9-095 with Rail Alphabet lettering.

"The BRUTE platform trolleys were painted Rail Blue, but post office trolleys were still GPO red." BRUTE: British Rail Universal Trolley Equipment. Letter mail for Travelling Post Offices was always handled by mailbag loads. It wasn't until *Railnet* that Royal Mail used a type of mini-BRUTEs that were known as *Yorks*, due to them first being trialled in that city.

Styling the Post Office

Double Arrow

In the DRU team, Gerry Barney devised the 'double-arrow' symbol which was used on trains, tickets, and signs, and survives as a railway designator today.

BR Sectorisation (Parcels)
From 1982, British Rail was organised into five divisions: InterCity, Network SouthEast, Regional Railways, Railfreight, and *Parcels*. Railfreight (1982-1987) split into six categories which were Coal, Construction, Distribution, General, Metals, and Petroleum. BR's *Rail Express Parcels* and *Red Star Parcels* were brands which persisted alongside Royal Mail's activities. Rail Express Parcels (Collection & Delivery), and Station to Station ceased c1981/2. BR had carried newspapers for all of the major distributors, but with new technology, the traditional hot-metal printing operations of Fleet Street relocated to Wapping, and other places where road transport won over rail. The last *Mirrors* were conveyed by rail from London in 1986. The final run of newspaper coaches was July 1988.

Night Mail
In 1986 the 50th anniversary of the Post Office's documentary *Night Mail* (1936), including WH Auden's famous verse, was celebrated. Six mail coaches were repainted from BR blue/grey into RM red livery with yellow double-line type *Royal Mail Letters*. [Later example shown below.]

Night Mail 2: 47515 Loco

80365 POS
80422 POT
80320 POS
80362 POS
80421 POT
80363 POS
80868 brake van.

A Mark I 80367 NSX, Travelling Post Office at Stafford 06/05/1988 © Steve Jones.
NSX is a TOPS code: Post Office Sorting Van - Dual air and vacuum braked.

Mail by Rail

Night Mail 2
In September 1986 filming of *Night Mail 2* featured the newly formed rake of TPO coaches, which also had specially painted red roofs to enhance overhead shots and was headed by 47515 in InterCity livery. *Night Mail 2* was produced by TVS - TV South (formerly Southern Television). The film included an updated poem by Blake Morrison, together with music by James Harpham. *Night Mail 2* was released commercially as part of a Post Office documentary *The Midnight Hours* (1987).

Loco Naming
On 25 September, locomotive 47515 was named *Night Mail* at Derby station by Bill Cockburn, MD of Royal Mail Letters. And on 26 September 47549 was named *Royal Mail* at London St. Pancras station by Sir Ronald Dearing, Chairman of the Post Office. Both 47515 and 47549 were still liveried as InterCity at that time.
These events effectively re-launched the red TPO livery and previewed the forthcoming business unit *Royal Mail Letters* which was formed in October 1986.

Parcels Sector red and grey

From about 1988 Parcels Sector class 47 locos were painted grey and red.

Left: A rather weathered loco 47476 Night Mail at Saltley © Steve Jones (1999).

The letter and parcel businesses were changing, and the Post Office was reviewing its policies of mail by rail. Rolling stock and locomotives were reallocated accordingly.

Styling the Post Office

Night Mail 3
A third railway poem was used to good effect in British Rail's corporate TV advert which was directed by Hugh Hudson with music by Vangelis. First shown 21:00 UK 25th December 1988.

"This commercial cleverly shows the enormous scale of BR's daily operation and the structure of the 'sectorised' business - Parcels, Railfreight, InterCity, Provincial and Network SouthEast. The opening sequence features the northbound Travelling Post Office with Auden's original verse, narrated by Sir Tom Courtenay. Auden's unique poetic style is then developed to underlie the freight, passenger, and station film sequences. The footage includes many of the railway's iconic structures including the Tyne, Forth and Saltash Bridges as well as the latest rolling stock, including the Wessex Electrics, introduced in May 1988."

Royal Mail Letters

Under Sectorisation, several *Parcels Express* DMU sets were fitted with roller shutters and rebranded as *Royal Mail* or *Royal Mail Letters*. British Rail was privatised following the Railways Act of 1993.

DMU class 114 54902 at Tyseley, Birmingham not long after conversion to a parcels unit from 54036. It had been fitted with roller doors and painted into Royal Mail red livery © Andy Cole 02/04/1988.

Royal Mail 1990

In 1990, Royal Mail introduced the 'Cruciform device' as part of its new corporate identity. The earlier *Banks and Miles* double-line typeface was retained for the yellow *Royal Mail* lettering. At the same time, the TPO font was changed to Stemple Garamond Italic, white lettering as pictured below.

Right: Carriage 'Brian White' at Nene Valley Railway © J. Chenery (2009).

Royal Mail Travelling Post Office in preservation at Nene Valley Railway © J. Chenery (2009). Note the small windows which had been a design feature of rolling stock since the Great Train Robbery.

Coincident with the change of corporate identity in 1990, TPO rolling stock was for the first time sign-written with the words *Royal Mail Travelling Post Office*, the previous unwillingness to advertise their function, following the 1963 Great Train Robbery, having been overcome.

The Apparatus

Use of apparatus (mechanism and net) to catch and despatch mailbags while travelling, ceased in October 1971, but sets in preservation retained the feature to demonstrate the process.

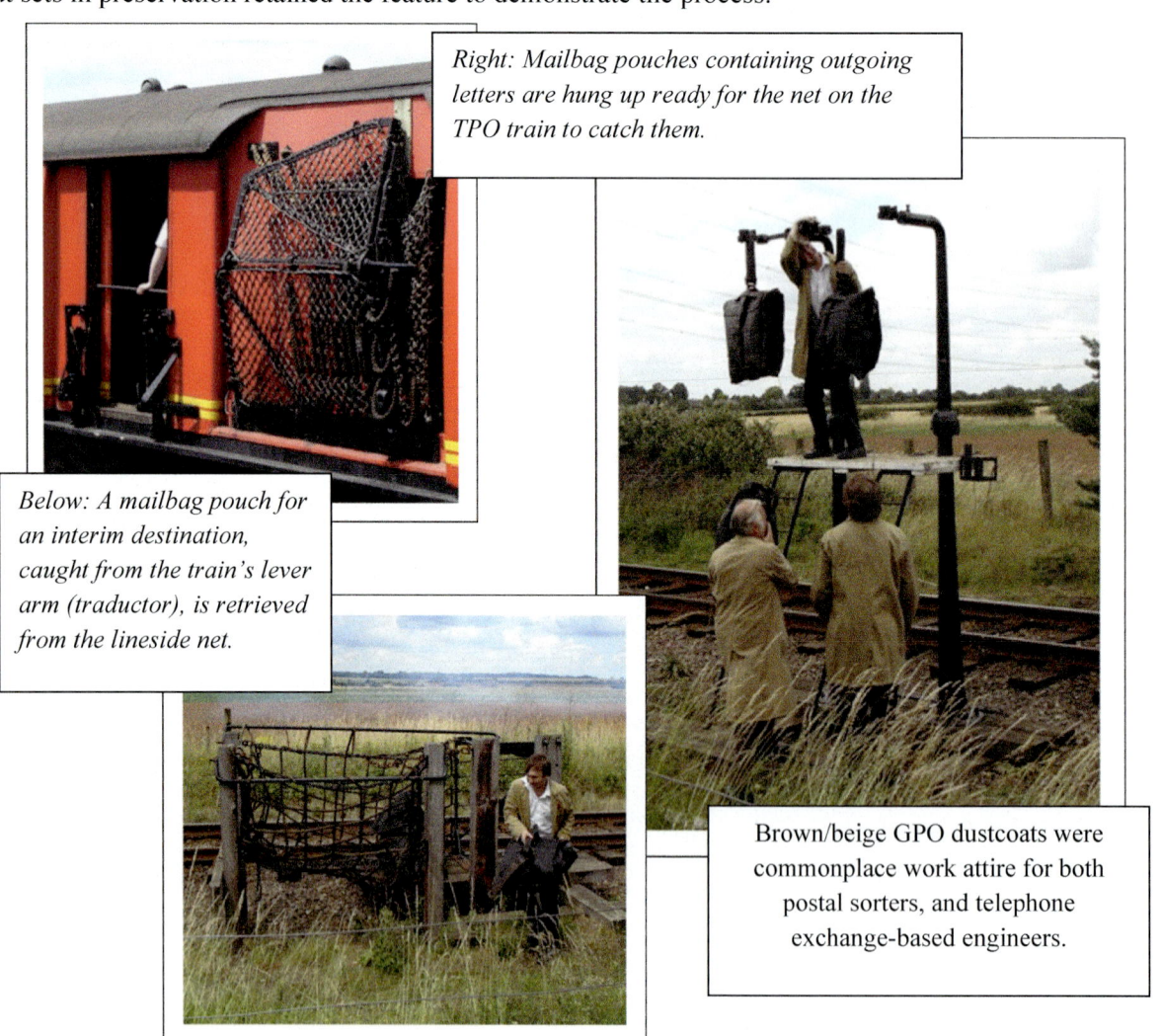

Right: Mailbag pouches containing outgoing letters are hung up ready for the net on the TPO train to catch them.

Below: A mailbag pouch for an interim destination, caught from the train's lever arm (traductor), is retrieved from the lineside net.

Brown/beige GPO dustcoats were commonplace work attire for both postal sorters, and telephone exchange-based engineers.

*Top left: Lever arms in doorway, and adjacent net on TPO coach.
Travelling Post Office demo at Nene Valley Railway © J. Chenery (2009).*

Mail by Rail

RES: Rail Express Systems (1991-1996)

In October 1991, the parcel carrying operations of British Rail became *Rail Express Systems* (*Res*). It is thought that the predominantly red livery was chosen because its major customer was the Post Office (Royal Mail). Res managed all parcels and letters traffic including TPOs.

"Res (Rail Express Systems) introduced a striking red livery with blue and grey flashes."

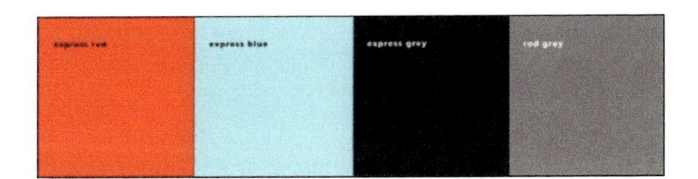

Res colours: express red, express blue, express grey, rod grey. [Reference: doublearrow.co.uk]

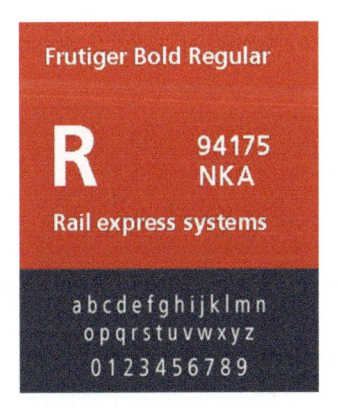

Frutiger font by Swiss designer, Adrian Frutiger.

NKA 94175 in Res livery at Stafford 13/08/2003 © Steve Jones. TOPS: NKA General Utility Van with hinged beams for BRUTE Traffic 90 mph or General Utility Van with Roller Shutter Doors 100 mph. A suffix is for Air braked.

The light blue rectangles of the Res logo were said to represent stacked parcels. A more surreal suggestion was that the light blue and grey flashes portrayed a set of stylised eagle's wings, conveying the speed element of the service.

RES

The 47/7 class Res locomotives were used on the higher profile mail jobs, primarily the TPO trains, because they were fitted with the appropriate multiple working gear to allow them to be moved with a Propelling Control Vehicle (PCV) at the opposite end of some of these trains. This left the Parcels sector the red class 47/4s working newspaper trains and bulk mail services.

Res carriages displayed the RM Cruciform and operated either as complete trains or in formations with *Royal Mail Travelling Post Office* branded POS (Post Office Sorters). The white font by Adrian Frutiger was released in 1976. Res was bought by EWS in 1996, but ultimately, Res branded stock was mostly redundant after 2003 when RM switched to road transport.

Railnet 1996

Royal Mail's commitment to moving mail-by-rail seemed assured following a project to concentrate mail interchange between road and rail at a number of new strategic, large mail-handling centres located away from passenger stations. For London specifically this was the PRDC (Princess Royal Distribution Centre) at Willesden opened on 30 September 1996.

Gone were the days of loading individual mail bags. The *York* trolleys/containers (mini-BRUTEs) were wheeled directly onto the trains. Each *York* held either mailbags or plastic trays of letters. The wide platforms allowed mechanical handling of multiple *Yorks*.

Mail trains 325011 and 325012 at PRDC with York containers in foreground © Paul David Smith (1998).

PRDC was developed by Broadway Malyan, for Royal Mail Property Holdings to contain seven platforms (taking 12-coach trains) with direct access to the WCML (West Coast Main Line). The road hub had 40 vehicle loading bays.

Mail by Rail

All mail operations from the mainline stations, Euston, Paddington, and Liverpool Street ceased upon transfer to the Willesden facility. PRDC covers 13,500 square metres. Other main hubs were located at Low Fell (Tyneside), Tonbridge, Warrington, Shieldmuir (Wishaw), Stafford, Bristol Parkway and Doncaster.

Railnet's 10-year contract with BR was ended prematurely as RM withdrew from 'mail by rail' in 2003. The last TPO trains ran on the night of 9 January 2004. Sorting letters on the move had become inefficient and potentially dangerous, due respectively to increased letter-sorting machine-technology, and problems with Railtrack (poor maintenance and timetable scheduling).

Class 325 Trains
A fleet of 16 dual-voltage (overhead and third rail) EMUs was commissioned by Royal Mail from ABB Ltd based at Derby, and these became the 325 class (325001-325016) exclusively for mail train duties to run between Railnet locations. Each 4 carriage set could accommodate 235 *Yorks* - a large volume of mail. Existing Res carriages were upgraded to accept *Yorks* too.

Above: A Railnet Stafford, box container.

EMU 325013 at Crewe 2010 © Steve Jones.
Note the double yellow lined chevron/vector which formed part of the 1990 Royal Mail motor vehicle branding.

Class 325 Trains

Left: EMU 325009

Passing through Rugby © Andy Cole (2020).

The double yellow lines have been removed to affect a simpler, less expensive brand to maintain.

Chris Hogan, Post Office Vehicle Club: *"The double yellow vectors on the 325xxx mail trains were removed at repaint from 2014 as part of a C6 overhaul."*

The unit 325006 was named (08/10/1998) *John Grierson* in tribute to the famous *Night Mail* verse and documentary of 1936. Each four-carriage formation of the 325s consists of:

DTPMV A: Driver Trailer Postal Mail Van A
MPMV: Motor Postal Mail Van
TPMV: Trailer Postal Mail Van
DTPMV B: Driver Trailer Postal Mail Van B

For various operational reasons the 325 units were often hauled by EWS locos. GB Railfreight picked up the failed RM contract in 2005. DB [Deutsche Bahn] Schenker bought EWS in 2007 and won back the mail contract in 2010. From 2016, DB Cargo UK became the licensed operator. Fifteen of the Class 325 units are still running; 325010 was damaged and later scrapped for spares.

2022: Railnet PRDC, Warrington, Shieldmuir, and Low Fell remain in use for mail services and Royal Mail is understood to be considering additions to its rail network in its quest to reach carbon-zero.

13: Royal Mail '90 to *Click. Drop. Done.*

> *'The new corporate identity is to position Royal Mail as a distinct and separate entity within The Post Office. The change of identity communicates to both employees and customers the beginning of a new era for Royal Mail.'*
> [POST 108/418 RM The New Corporate Identity.]

Following the re-org in 1986 the Post Office had four main business units: Letters, Parcels, PO Counters, and National Girobank. As the 1990s approached, it was obvious that to develop the individual trading units, a separate identity would be needed for each. It was intended to sell-off Girobank, and this was purchased by Alliance & Leicester in July 1990. Initially, the letters business wanted to establish a new identity, with the potential to show different levels of service for its mail portfolio:

"The development of our own identity is an important way in which we can help differentiate Royal Mail to our customers." [POST 108/418 RM The New Corporate Identity.]

Barry Robinson, the established Design Adviser for the Post Office, invited *Sedley Place* into the project to formulate a new concept image that would distinguish the Royal Mail brand. *Sedley Place* subsequently presented a diagrammatic representation of its design ideas. The iconic *Banks and Miles, Royal Mail* yellow on red typeface was retained, and a white backing panel was added upon which to display the crown. The white panel could potentially change colour, to bronze, silver, or gold, and with additional text, be used to denote tiered levels of letter mail, service offerings.

The initial presentation to Royal Mail was misunderstood to be the finished identity, rather than a starting point for a more complex design, and thus the project was handed over to *SampsonTyrrell* for their interpretation of the client's requirements.

In the event, the envisaged tiered service levels weren't introduced, but *SampsonTyrrell* was still expected to pick up the incomplete design concept and implement a finished, practical identity that would faithfully represent the Royal Mail brand.

Styling the Post Office

SampsonTyrrell (later WPP)
Graphic designers Terry Tyrrell and Sam Sampson formed *SampsonTyrrell* in May 1976. Possibly as a media statement, the company name was styled without a space between the two words.
Decades later the naming of *openreach* followed a different trend of all-lower-case letters.

Sarah Stevens recalls her work in the late 1980s:

"I was privileged to be part of the team at SampsonTyrrell who created the new Royal Mail corporate identity. When we were briefed, the Royal Mail cruciform logo had already been designed by Sedley Place but there were concerns that it was expensive to reproduce – it included printing with gold and silver inks! The solution was to develop photographic stylised images of the St. Edward's and Scottish Crowns which were digitised and are still in use today."

The Scottish logo was distinguished by use of the Scottish Crown in place of the St. Edward's Crown. For the Welsh logo the words 'Royal Mail' were translated to 'Post Brenhinol.'

Scan: A book of first class stamps – the numerals are styled in Stempel Garamond, and the St. Edward's Crown forms part of the cruciform device.

Terence Griffin who had worked for *Sedley Place* explained that *The Post Office* was to split letters/parcels to be able to compete with upcoming carriers such as DHL, and others, hence the separate business units in 1986, and the requirement for them all to have new identities.

Quote from leaflets*: 'The livery has been standardised through the use of Royal Mail Red, the application of the relevant cruciform logo, and the Royal Cypher to all vehicle doors. The half-arrow device, comprised of Double Line stripes, has been developed solely for use on vehicles. Projecting a modern, dynamic image for the business, it is applied wherever the vehicle moulding allows.' [A Manager's Guide to using Royal Mail's Identity.]*

Fonts
Stempel Garamond was chosen as the typeface because of its prestigious appearance, legibility, and wide availability.

Royal Mail '90

The corporate typeface was specified as: Stempel Garamond Roman, Italic, Bold, and Bold Italic.

Sign at Mount Pleasant in Stempel Garamond typeface © J. Chenery (2006).

Royal Mail
The yellow chevron logo:

A 1990 Royal Mail Leyland-DAF van H725 OKG. Serial 0081158 © Mike Street (July 1991).

Campaign: Please use the Postcode. [Typeface is white Stempel Garamond italic].

Sarah Stevens recalls: *"Many, many ideas for the Royal Mail vehicles were presented. It was a difficult task with numerous stakeholders involved. Eventually, a design that included the double yellow stripe was selected – the stripe comes from the Royal Mail lettering in the logo and was thought of by Royal Mail as a key equity graphic element.*

The double yellow stripe formed a chevron arrow pointing to the front of the vehicle on both sides of the van, with the Royal Mail logo contained within it. It was hoped the arrow shape would enable Royal Mail to shift their perception of being slow, backward, and bureaucratic to forward-thinking and dynamic."

Parcelforce

Newell and Sorrell won the contract and created the first Parcelforce logo.

Parcelforce became the trading name of Royal Mail Parcels in August 1990.

Left: Early Parcelforce liveried Leyland DAF H859 CHW with Royal Mail name still included © Mike Street (1991).

Right: Leyland Roadrunner C378 YNF RM Parcels in Banks and Miles lettering © Mike Street (1986).

In 1997 the business was rebranded to Parcelforce Worldwide.

Left: Ford Transit 350 Trend YM14 OXC PFWW van Express Worldwide Delivery © J. Chenery (2017).

Early *Parcelforce* branding included the *Royal Mail* name, and some vans retained the royal cypher on the cab door, for a short while.

End of the Double-Line Vector

Left: Vauxhall Combo 2005 EA05 VRR with yellow double-line vector © J. Chenery (July 2011).

Note how the red paint fades towards a pink shade after years of sun exposure.

Below: Vauxhall Combo 2006 EA06 VFH © J. Chenery (Sept 2010).

In 2005 Royal Mail needed cost savings to offset its pension deficit and to prepare for increased competition from 2006.

A simplified livery without yellow stripes was part of the economy measures.

Chris Hogan, Post Office Vehicle Club: *"The removal of the yellow vectors from the specification was a 2005 economy measure by RM Fleet; the 587xxxx Transit Connects were the first affected. The corresponding vectors on the 325xxx mail trains were removed at repaint from 2014 as part of a C6 overhaul."*

New vehicle deliveries from 2006 were specified without the vector, which had been a feature of the RM identity since 1990. Existing vehicles with the old logo were left unchanged until end of life.

Styling the Post Office

Evolving the Brand
Here are just a few of the typeface branding changes over the years. The subtleties of stamp design and the colour updates in the logos on the booklets is a whole other topic! The corporate font specified in 1990 was Stempel Garamond. On stamp books some years after 2000, (date not known) this reverted to Helvetica.

Helvetica, a sans-serif typeface was developed in 1957 by Swiss designers Max Miedinger and Eduard Hoffmann.

Helvetica numerals and text.

Chevin 2007
A new corporate typeface was adopted for both Royal Mail and the Post Office. In 2003 Nick Cooke had developed Chevin, which he named after a hill near his home in West Yorkshire. The design wasn't specifically intended for Royal Mail group, but presumably its clear, less formal style was suited to a more accessible, easy to deal with, company.

The new typeface Chevin was not applied to stamp books until 2016.

Entrance sign at Mount Pleasant © J. Chenery (2019).

Royal Mail's all-embracing use of Chevin extended to its electronic document templates which were used to maintain branding, for example when creating customer presentations. In 2012 RM reverted some Office documents to Arial because Chevin wasn't a fully supported embedded font when sending documents outside of the business. Compatibility across all media has become such an important factor in brand design and deployment.

CLICK. DROP. DONE.

> Historically, the sides of RM vans would have carried advertising boards.
>
> In the 2010s this was somewhat mitigated by simple inclusion of the web address www.royalmail.com
>
> *Fiat Doblò in RM livery © J. Chenery (2016).*

Click & Drop was first launched in 2015.

CLICK DROP DONE in bold Chevin capitals.

In Chevin lower case:
Download the app.
Convenient,
trusted UK and
global parcel delivery

Royal Mail Peugeot Expert KM21 NRK. Serial 20981686 © J. Chenery (2021).

Click. Drop. Done. was Royal Mail's slogan for its online postage shop at www.royalmail.com. CLICK the webpage to buy postage, print the label and DROP the letter or parcel at a Delivery Office, Post Office, or pillar box. DONE.

Zero Emission Electric Vehicles (EVs)

Increasingly, more service vehicles had a yellow and red hatched area on the rear doors to warn motorists when stopped or parked at the roadside on deliveries.

Zero Emission Electric Vehicle in white Chevin font.

The 2019 registered EVs had a dual (unzipped) livery of RM red one side, the remainder being a new lime green as the environmentally greener vehicles were gradually revealed. Subsequent EVs had a single *Currant Red* finish.

Photos: Mercedes-Benz eVito electric van at Mount Pleasant © J. Chenery (2019).

The 'unzipped' vans were liveried with Mediafleet's colour coating system, called WrapidCoat. The special branding covered 190 vans as part of a media campaign to introduce EVs into Royal Mail.

14.1: The Post Office

The Post Office had been in existence seemingly forever. To some people, it was still the GPO (General Post Office). Few people understood the significance of its name(s), or the inter-related hierarchy of its organisation. Royal Mail delivered the post, but letters were sent at the Post Office? Even within its own ranks the correct marketing names for each function were sometimes a cause for debate. Regardless of what the public thought, the GPO had ceased to exist in 1969 when the organisation became the Post Office corporation.

In 1981, British Telecom (originally Post Office Telephones) had completely separated from the top-level parent company known then as the Post Office. Brand consultants and designers, *Banks and Miles* had devised a new typeface for British Telecom which allowed it to transition into a plc, all with minimal effort. Historically, from 1975 the Post Office (postal and telecoms) had a single unified brand and company, using the *Post Office Double Line* typeface which *Banks and Miles* had previously worked so hard to design for them.

Strangely, the Post Office monogram (sometimes referred to as the crest}, was used across the company, right up until 1981 when the *Post Office Double Line* type was finally used on the Report and Accounts for that year.

In 1981 the monogram changed to the PO Double Line typeface as a corporate ID.

Going forward, British Telecom and the Post Office needed to prepare for the ensuing competitive marketplaces that they were soon to face as their monopoly advantages would inevitably be eroded. In 1986 the creation of Letters, Parcels, and Counters, business units within the Post Office enabled them to focus on different aspects of the market and to tailor their products more directly to their customers. This had involved the development of separate brand identities, but what of the Post Office as the parent corporation?

Styling the Post Office

"The Post Office had to change from a single all-embracing organisation, hence the creation of Post Office Counters, Parcelforce, and Royal Mail as separate business entities, each with their own identity."
[A Manager's Guide to using Royal Mail's Identity.]

The once prominent *Banks and Miles* branding was gradually being displaced by new ideas, as the Post Office moved forward with its agenda to become a far different organisation. The Royal Mail '90 branding of businesses established a need for a new logo for the Post Office at top-level. At this stage, Royal Mail was just one of the emerging brands which sat under the Post Office name and was to do so for another ten years.

A New Corporate Logo c1991

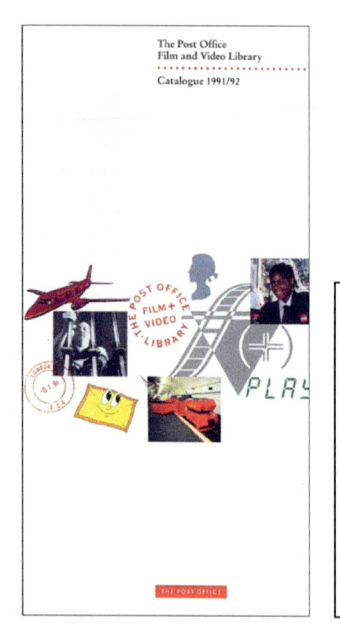

This corporate logo wasn't normally seen on the street nor in transactions at post office counters.

Sedley Place was established by Gerry Barney, David Bristow, Kit Cooper, and Terence Griffin in 1977. Their company had a long relationship with the Post Office. Sedley Place had done the initial design of the Royal Mail cruciform, and although they didn't develop that idea further themselves, they were asked to create a new branding for the top-level Post Office identity.

Scan of: The Post Office Film and Video Library Catalogue 1991/92 showing (bottom centre) the new corporate logo.

The Post Office
With the Postal Services Act 2000, the Post Office corporation became a public limited company on 26 March 2001 and was renamed Consignia plc. Ownership remained with the Crown. At this point the long-established name Post Office, as the parent company, was swept away.

14.2: Consignia

Consignia (2001-2002)

This new name was one of several options promulgated by consultancy firm Dragon Brands and was introduced by the Post Office's chief executive John Roberts on 9 January 2001 as *"modern, meaningful and entirely appropriate."* The name was officially adopted from 26 March 2001. The establishment of Postcomm – the Postal Services Commission was to oversee the licensing and regulation of all postal service operators, as market competition would gradually step up.

The Post Office needed a new brand to enable it to easily trade overseas. Observers commented that an additional, new trading subsidiary would have satisfied the requirements, but the Post Office decided to change the top level brand in one move, which unfortunately proved detrimental to its corporate reputation.

It's conjectured that *Consignia* was invented to give a meaning of consigning or entrusting a letter or package to the company for delivery. Also, *signia* a possible shortening of insignia, for a symbol of power, playing on the heritage of Royal Mail. The new name would have formed the basis of a modern international brand with the aspirations of a company needing to compete in the marketplace.

Neither the name, concept or symbol was properly explained or understood by the public or press, who may have thought that the long-established Post Office/Royal Mail would be no more.

Consignia – The new name for The Post Office Group.
The project team: *"We had a budget of £1.9M...the logo was drawn...the little swirly thing was all designed."*

John Roberts CEO of Consignia suggested that the actual cost of the name change had only been £0.5M, the remainder being associated with converting to a public limited company.
Creative agency Rufus Leonard was founded in 1989 by partners who had formerly worked for Wolff Olins. Rufus Leonard was tasked by Consignia to update its web presence after the Post Office Group was renamed. Notably, in 1998 Rufus Leonard took part in the creation of one of the most dynamic adverts – the *'Yellow Pages Tube Train'* which was a normal working train wrapped in bright yellow, displaying YP advertising which included specially upholstered matching seats.

Michele Carter, who had also worked for Wolff Olins, set up *August Associates Management for Designers* with Simon May. Because of their management skills they were asked to implement the Royal Mail to Consignia rebrand.

The End of Consignia

Subsequently, *Royal Mail* as a top-level legal entity was created on 4 November 2002 because in use the name Consignia was perceived to be so unpopular with customers and the media. Company number 4138203 was renamed from Consignia plc to Royal Mail Group plc.

The words Post Office couldn't be registered as a unique identity abroad, therefore it was decided to reassign the already well-respected *Royal Mail* brand, to become the new top-level company name. All the Consignia branding had to be replaced by Royal Mail at a further cost of another million pounds. This may have included stationery, building signs, corporate clothing, computer software, and more, although it's not known how pervasively the Consignia images had already been rolled out. Regardless of the top-level name, the Royal Mail brand for the postal service, and sub-brand, Parcelforce Worldwide would have continued, at least for the immediate future.

Due to the intention of the Government to eventually privatise the postal business, the legal names went through a complex transition from Consignia to Royal Mail Holdings to variants of Royal Mail. Finally, Royal Mail was floated on the Stock Market as Royal Mail plc on 15 October 2013.

International Distributions Services Plc

On 3 October 2022 the holding company Royal Mail plc was renamed *International Distributions Services plc*.

Post Office Counters

Throughout the Royal Mail Group changes within the Post Office and Royal Mail, the *Post Office Counters'* business unit was still the place where customers visited a post office to buy stamps and to post letters and parcels.
Post Office Counters Ltd remained under government control and was demerged from Royal Mail Group on 1 April 2012, as Post Office Limited (POL); the only part of the once great General Post Office to retain the name.

15: Post Office Counters

The entity Post Office Counters Ltd was created in 1987 to encompass and manage the established network of post offices which served the public. The brand inherited elements of the *Banks and Miles* double-line lettering, corporate style which had first been developed in the 1970s. In the decades that followed, Post Office Counters refreshed its branding periodically, with changes of colour, typeface, and styles in an ongoing evolution of the identity.

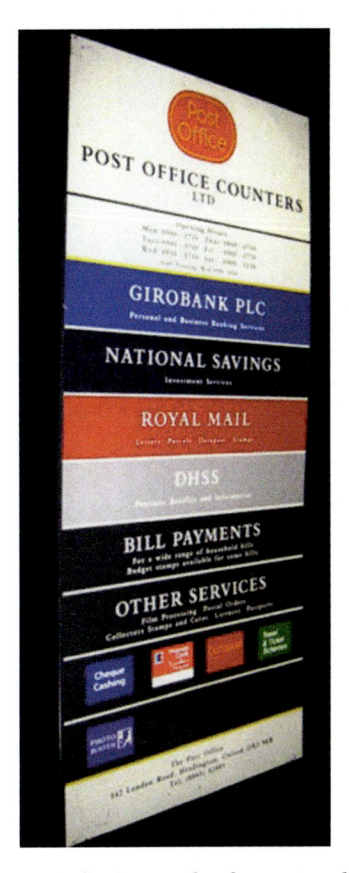

The simple exterior design uses only the 'Post Office oval' and a multi-informational board to identify the branch.

Southend-on-Sea BO at 199 High Street, opened 1993, relocated 2017
© J. Chenery
(March 1993).

Left: *A typical informational board showing services available. Ref: 2002-0889/1 © The Postal Museum 2022.*
Right: *Southend-on-Sea BO at 199 High Street, opened 1993, relocated 2017 © J. Chenery, March 1993.*

Styling the Post Office

1993 Branding
As part of the Post Office's gearing up for postal competition, it started to rebrand its operating businesses into unique brands. During the 1990s, *Newell and Sorrell*, and later *SampsonTyrrell* developed the signage and colour palettes into a refreshed but complementary look. The iconic oval-shaped external sign took on a distinctly different appearance to that of the *Banks and Miles'* era. The new turquoise green colour scheme was unlike anything tried before!

Newell and Sorrell was founded in 1976 by Frances Newell and John Sorrell.

In 1997 the company became Interbrand Newell and Sorrell, owned by Omnicom, as leading design firms merged into influential players in the industry.

Top: The new branding for the 1990s, at Barnstaple Post Office © Malcolm Jones (2009).
Left: G174 NRM (9610068) was a one-off, special conversion in 1996 of a Leyland Roadrunner (registered 5/90) into a Mobile Post Office using the livery of the period, at Carlisle Motor Transport Workshop (MTW) © Mike Street (19/08/1998).

1993 Branding

The Design Standards Volume 1 dated Jan 1997 defined the typefaces to be used as Gill Sans, Joanna, and Palatino.

Colours: Post Office Counters' Red, Yellow, Green, and Cream.

Red: Pantone 186, RAL 3020 Traffic Red.
Yellow: Pantone 109, RAL 1018 Zinc Yellow.
Green: Pantone 341, RAL 6016 Turquoise Green.
Cream: Pantone 9180, BS4800/5252 10 B 15 Cream/Ivory.

The green banding remained for some time after the corporate image had moved onto the next iteration of red and white.

Right: Ford Transit DY05 HVS in Essex © J. Chenery (2012). 'Post Office delivering value.' 08457 740 740
www.royalmail.com

Thieves Beware: Smartwater (property marking)

Cashier No. 3 Please!

Undoubtedly one of the most innovative and memorable queuing systems was first introduced into crown post offices in the mid-1990s. Devised and personally voiced by Terry Green, his *Qmatic* CFM (Customer Flow Management) announcements are still in use today.

Horizon (1999)

The *Horizon* computer software system, developed by Fujitsu, for the daily management of transactions at post office counters, was introduced in 1999. Sadly, due to faulty programming and senior management denial, this had the most detrimental effect on the running of branches and the integrity of the Post Office and its staff.

Ultimately it ruined the lives of many hundreds of its people (and their families), through wrongful prosecutions for fraud which are only now (2021) being righted.

Post Office Ltd
On 1 October 2001 Post Office Counters Ltd was renamed Post Office Ltd.

National Archives: '*Post Office Ltd absorbed the Post Office Network, Network Banking, Cash Handling and Distribution, Customer Management (Government unit) business units in Royal Mail and all of their functions, in addition to the brands, network and functions of Post Office Counters Ltd.*'

2007 Branding
Network Change in 2007 was an initiative to close 2,500 branches to optimise the size of the network and stem losses. From 2010 *Network Transformation* was rationalising the remaining post offices into Crown, Main, and Locals. These programmes may have prompted the return to the more traditional red and white colour scheme.

The new look for 2007, at Poulton Post Office, Market Square © Malcolm Jones (2010). The text postoffice.co.uk on the fascia board is Chevin font. The pillar boxes are Type K.

Post Office Counters

POL (2012)
On 1 April 2012, Post Office Limited (POL) was demerged from Royal Mail Group.

Proba Pro 2014
This new typeface, a geometric sans was designed by Andriy Konstantynov and first published in May 2014 at the *Mint Type* foundry. The Post Office licensed its use, and it was widely specified.

> *Shopfront Guide October 2021:*
> *"At the Post Office we use Proba Pro because it's clear and straightforward, but not boring."*

Redder
From about 2014 brighter and graduated reds were trialled to enhance the brand.

> The brand continues to evolve every few years as the Post Office solicits attention in an ever more competitive marketplace. Long gone are the days of it being solely a service for the public, which automatically got their business.
>
> Pantone 186C red and 427C stone were specified for the surround of the cash machines, specifically the Wincor-Nixdorf 2050 ATM (Automatic Teller Machine).
>
> 'Free Cash withdrawals & balance enquiries.'
> 'This ATM is owned & operated by Post Office.'

Post Office Network (branches)
The Post Office is mandated by the government to maintain a network of at least 11,500 outlets in order to receive its ongoing financial support. At the end of March 2021, the network comprised of 9646 agency branches, 1,651 outreach services, and 118 crown offices.

By comparison in 2013 there were 373 crown offices, which were mostly the larger branches, and all staffed by Post Office employees. Some crown offices had a philatelic bureau within purpose-built premises. The traditional model is gradually being eroded as more services move online, and options such as Royal Mail's *Parcel Collect* (launched October 2020) and *Click & Drop* negate a visit to the post office.

2014 Branding

Crown office at 205 Old Street, London, EC1 © Chris Downer (2020). The text postoffice.co.uk on the fascia board is Chevin font, and this was new branch signage fitted during 2014.

Stamp Vending Machines (SVMs)

Post Office SVMs dispensing books of 12 first or second class stamps.

The *Thomas 6002* electronic SVMs were manufactured by Thomas Automation Ltd of Loughborough, which traded from 1972 until circa 2013. The company specialised in coin-operated machines.

Produced from 2002 in the turquoise finish which related to the 1993 Post Office Counters (POC) brand, these SVMs were later covered in red vinyl to match the new 2007 POC identity which included Chevin typeface. Unlike previous SVMs they were managed by Post Office Counters rather than Royal Mail.

*Left: SVM at Bedale Market Place, North Yorkshire
© Post Box on Flickr CC2.0 (Mar 2009).*

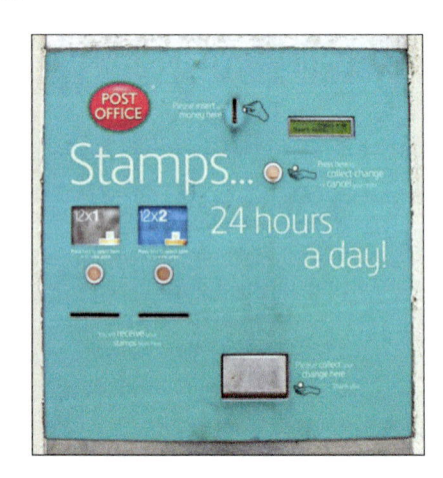

SVMs

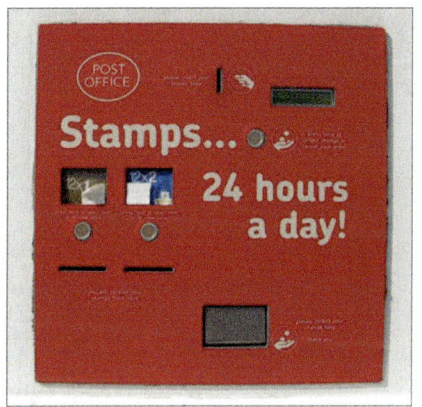

…please insert your money here.

…press here to collect change or cancel your order.

…press here to select item or view price.

…you will receive your stamps from here.

…please collect your change here. thank you.

Left: Thomas 6002 Stamp vending machine in Felixstowe © Dave Bullock (Sept 2009).

Post and Go

Full self-service suites are rather ambitious compared to simple stamp vending. Unlike the machines of the 1960s, the current software driven screen prompts make it almost as easy as self- checkout at the supermarket! An understanding of *Pricing in Proportion* (introduced 2006), which replaced pricing by weight alone is desirable.

Above: Post and Go at The Postal Museum, Clerkenwell © J. Chenery (2022).

Left: Post and Go (full service suite), in Sheffield © Malcolm Jones (2019).

Styling the Post Office

Left: Merc Sprinter WR19 UXA in Post Office livery at Clerkenwell © J. Chenery (2019).
POST OFFICE as Proba Pro font, and Postoffice.co.uk in Chevin font.

Brand Refresh 2020 with Coley Porter Bell
In August 2022 Simon Marshall (Head of Brand) kindly gave an overview of some recent styling. With the intension of moving away from *Proba Pro*, and *Chevin* typefaces, they now had an exclusive font, *Post Office Headline* which was designed by Dalton Maag. [This was the same foundry that had developed fonts for BT.] POL vehicles delivered since 2021 use *Post Office Headline* lettering together with *Nunito Sans Extra Bold* for the subsidiary wording.

The oval-shaped post office sign, which for so many decades had distinguished the counters part of the business, was immortalised into a new typeface for the brand, circa 2020. Type foundry, Dalton Maag used the oval sign as inspiration for elongated lettering, which was developed into *Post Office Headline*, literally forged from the heritage story.

Top right: 'We're here to help' leaflet in Post Office Headline type. FSR 57/21 April 2021.

Left: Dalton Maag's 2010 Aktiv Grotesk sans-serif typeface was reshaped into Post Office Headline. Note especially, the elongated letter e.

Post Office Counters

Design agency Coley Porter Bell (CPB) collaborated to engage freelance conceptual illustrator Tom Peake. CPB is part of WPP (Wire and Plastic Products 1971) which is one of the world's leading advertising and marketing companies, that includes Ogilvy.

Tom's illustrative poster-like drawings, depicting everyday people at the Post Office, are as iconic as some of the work commissioned back in the 1930s when Sir Stephen Tallents was the public relations officer of the Post Office.

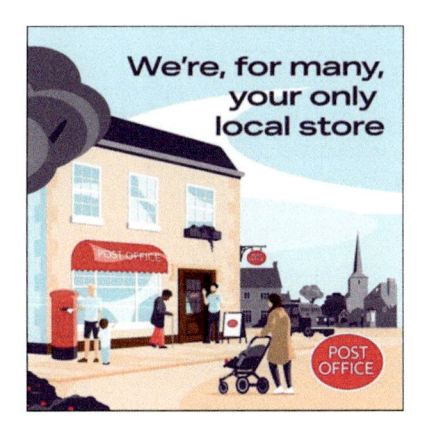

Tom Peake illustrator produced wonderfully timeless depictions of everyday people going to the Post Office. The text uses the new 'Post Office Headline' font.

Drawings sourced from Twitter: 'Abbey Road Post Office' July 2021.

"We've had superb feedback from our Postmasters. They think its fresh and modern whilst nodding to our heritage." Simon Marshall, Head of Brand, Post Office.

Campaigns

Post Office marketing is a never ending task to be, fresh, original, and engaging. Here's just one memorable example:

In 2001 London agency *Publicis* ran a campaign entitled *'The Post Office: What a Good Idea.'*

The ethos was to highlight post office services, such as currency exchange, that potential customers may not have realised were available.

This screen grab from the TV advert uses the 1993 oval-sign branding together with the campaign message.

Styling the Post Office

WHS Franchise

WH Smith has operated post offices in its stores since 2006. Many former crown post offices, larger offices run by the Post Office, were put out to franchise with WHS.

Southend's Crown Post Office moved into WHS in March 2017 and was then franchised in January 2019. The shop front POST OFFICE is Proba Pro typeface. Photo © J. Chenery (2019).

Bank Hub (2021)

In April 2021 the first ever BankHubs launched in Cambuslang, Lanarkshire and Rochford, Essex as part of the Community Access to Cash Pilots (CACP) initiative. The BankHubs provide customers with basic banking and cash services, as well as dedicated rooms where they can see advisers from their own bank.

BankHUB in West Street, Rochford
© 'saxonessex on Flickr' (2021).

16: BT '91 and Beyond

BT today newspaper: *"BT needs to feel like, sound like, and behave like a quite different organisation from the one that emerged from the Post Office at the beginning of the 1980s."*

At the end of March 1991, a special supplement of *BT today* the newspaper for BT people introduced a new logo.

Wolff Olins…
Six design companies made proposals for BT's new corporate image, which was launched to the press on 20 March 1991.
The winning consultant, Wolff Olins explained branding as: *"…making everything in and around the company, its products, buildings and communications consistent in purpose, performance…and appearance."*

To develop all of these elements coherently takes time, which is why BT's Corporate Design Unit worked for three and a half years, writing and executing the brief with Wolff Olins.

BT Piper

Thus in April 1991, to engage its potential worldwide market, BT became the new simplified trading name of British Telecommunications plc. The government no longer had any (significant) financial holding in BT, but the company had to trade within the guidelines set out by the (then) regulatory body OFTEL (Office of Telecommunications) which was appointed by the government. In December 2003 OFTEL became OFCOM with a wider remit across the industry.

The new *Piper* logo symbolised the 'listening and speaking' concepts of communication. To the uninformed, it was the 'prancing piper,' and the true concept perhaps was not fully appreciated.

Styling the Post Office

Peter Denmark was the graphic illustrator who drew the BT Piper. Such was the affinity of the company with the symbol that Neil Lawson Baker was commissioned by chairman Iain Vallance to produce a large bronze sculpture of the piper in 3D for his London office.

Development of the Fleet 1991

The BT Fleet of vehicles gradually lost the long-established bright yellow safety colour in favour of a pale BT Grey. The white (almost ghostly) piper on the side of the vans was reflective to show up in car headlights.

Right: BT Transit van at Milton Keynes © J. Chenery (1999).

Stewart Signs

Artwork in the form of 3M™ Controltac™ vinyl transfers was developed by long-established vehicle wrapping specialist Stewart Signs. BT Corporate Logotype including ownership mark. Typestyle was Helvetica, weights 65/75/85. The white piper used specially formed reflective tape.

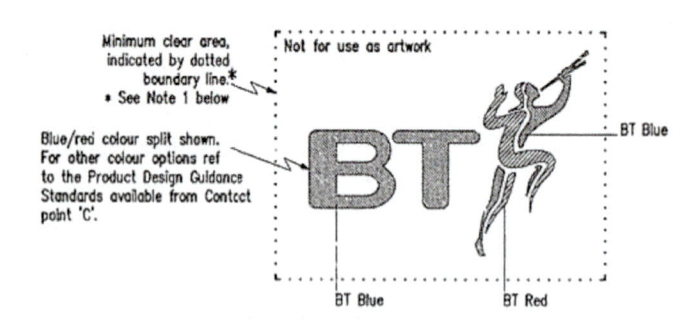

BT Red: Pantone 207c
BT Blue: Pantone 300c

PANTONE ® is a registered trademark of Pantone Inc.

From document drawing CN11617 23/1/92 via THGR.

"The legal title of the Company is British Telecommunications plc (upper and lower case text as written). This is unaffected by the April 1991 changes to the Corporate Identity. The abbreviated text 'British Telecom' or 'British Telecom plc' must <u>not</u> be used under any circumstances."

BT '91

Piper Variations

BT Piper (left): The 1991 colours of blue and red.

Post Office and British Telecom colours were mostly specified as British Standard paint colours. Pantone's colour matching scheme was devised in 1963. The new BT logos from 1991 adopted the design-industry pantone colour standard which allowed more accurate matching across a range of materials.

Photo: A KX100 style kiosk of the BT Piper era © J. Chenery 2006. KX telephone kiosks were designed by DCA (David Carter Associates) and produced by GKN. An all grey logo was used for the BT Piper on some kiosk enclosures.

1999 Branding

In October 1998, design group *Enterprise IG* (incorporating *SampsonTyrrell*) won the pitch to refresh the *look and feel* of the BT brand, against Wolff Olins, Interbrand Newell and Sorrell, and The Identica Partnership.

BT Piper (right): The stronger, darker red and blue of the later 1999 version.

Head of BT design, David Mercer: *"In effect, Enterprise IG takes over from Wolff Olins, which we have worked with for the past ten years."* Enterprise IG managing creative director Franco Bonadio: *"Our job will be to take the 'grey' out of BT. It is a leader and its should look like one."*

Styling the Post Office

KX100 + and Street Hubs
The KX100 + kiosk (1994) was also designed by DCA and manufactured by GKN and the first one was installed in London in August 1996.

Left: A group of less than salubrious KX100 + kiosks near St. Paul's London © J. Chenery (2022).

From 2017 BT with InLinkUK began to deploy advertising screens which had phone functionality (inc. 999 access), USB charging points and free wi-fi.

Right: A modern BT Street Hub screen in Holborn © J. Chenery (2019).

The KX series of kiosks had an aluminium frame clad with stainless steel panels. The additional standard features of the KX100 + were a red domed roof giving extra internal light and external visibility; Lower door handles for children and the disabled; A seat rest; A writing/parcel shelf; Larger and back-lit notices. A conversion kit allowed the basic KX100 to be fitted with a red domed roof. Particularly in London, the aim was to make the kiosk more reminiscent of the bygone era when red phone boxes were dominant. The dome of the KX 100+ kiosk on the far right has been further modified to incorporate a wi-fi hotspot.
BT bought out the existing InLinkUK network in 2019 and these are now marketed as Street Hubs. Advertising to fund the units is provided by Global Media Group Services Ltd.

Concert

BT's JV with MCI in 1994 and later with AT & T was not entirely successful and finally ended in 2001.

BT '91

1999 Branding

BT Internet
http://www.btinternet.com

BT Internet via dial-up modems was first available in March 1996 for consumers. It included an e-mail service and web space too.

David Mercer Head of Design (BT): *"We need to build on our heritage of trust and service, exemplified in the identity. The logo's background will be changed from grey to white to show off the trumpeting figure more effectively."*

Specialist body shells (photo left) from Anglian Developments, fitted out by Papworth Industries, were to prevail for many years. Variations of the Piper shape were devised for each van model.

Added van markings were: **www.bt.com and FreeFone 0800 800 800.**

The change from grey to a white van base-colour meant the end of special paint finishes.

The white fleet was introduced in December 1999 with a darker red and blue BT Piper.

Top: Ford Transit with Anglian bodywork by Papworth Industries (July 2000). Above: Ford Transit panel van (Mar 2003). Photos © J. Chenery.

Openworld 2000

The BT Openworld globe device was launched in April 2000 as the logo for *"the mass market internet business focused increasingly on broadband services."*

Adam Oliver gives his understanding of the Openworld globe as a corporate ID:

"The Openworld globe was created to articulate the 'dialling-up tone', the connection of a modem, spinning around [modulated tone], which is why it was animated. It was originally devised for Openworld and then when BT Group was considering a new group wide logo, they thought that the Openworld logo would be perfect, and that as they already owned the design it could be promoted to a company-wide logo. I found out via a conversation with one of the design companies for the Openworld logo that it caused a lot of annoyance for them, who otherwise would have charged a lot more for a company-wide logo."

Dial-up internet was widely available in 2000 but was starting to be superseded by 'always-on' broadband connections, typically ADSL. In 2004, *BT Broadband,* now delivered via ADSL technology, was rebranded *BT Yahoo* as the packages were enhanced. From 2020 the *BT Yahoo* e-mail users were gradually migrated back to a *BT Mail* platform.
ISP Preview reported that from 1 July 2022 BT would not offer new customers e-mail.

2003 Branding
Subsequently, the BT Openworld, 'connected world' globe logo was introduced 7 April 2003 as part of BT's new company-wide corporate image.

BT's Head of Design, David Mercer: *"The identity refresh project, although led by the brand and reputation team, was very much a cross-divisional exercise."*

A larger logo of the six coloured spheres, together with BT lettering was used on early deployments of the new brand.

Left: Ford Transit van with oversized BT 'Connected world' globe © J. Chenery (2010).

2003 Branding

As a logo, the 'connected world' globe was in use between 2000 and 2019.

Left: Vauxhall Vivaro van © J. Chenery (2010).

Below: BT Local Business Mini © D.A. Cott.

Openworld Globe:

Left: Component parts of the Openworld globe in a display case at BT Archives © J. Chenery (Jan 2018).

Adam Oliver: *"The sculpture was removed from the CEO's office when the new * BT logo came in. It was very carefully taken away and reassembled!"* [* BT Circle logo developed between 2016/19.]

Special Liveries

BT Local Business was set-up in 2002. BT's TV service via broadband established *BT Sport* as one of its premium channels. *BTFS* was the operating division of BT's estates management arm.

Styling the Post Office

Later Vehicles
BT Globe-badged vehicles acquired the ***Get in touch*** message with a less fussy web address of bt.com (without the www). Rear-end safety chevrons became the requirement for safer roadside working.

BT Facility Services (BTFS)
Building Services support, previously operated under Monteray, was bought back into the BT Group as BT Facility Services (BTFS) in September 2012. This resulted in the creation of yet another variation of BT branding for the division. In February 2022, 300 staff from BTFS were about to be TUPE'd to GXO Logistics as part of a longer term strategy.

Above: BT – 'Get in touch bt.com'
© J. Chenery (2019).

Right: Fiat Doblò van marked BTFS Facility Services part of BT
© J. Chenery (2014).

Far right: The more developed BTFS livery
© J. Chenery (2021).

BT 2012

In 2019, Franklin of *Red&White* [redandwhitestudio.com] wrote *"The [BT] brand has actually been purple for seven years, but customer research showed that people think it's blue."*

BT's use of purple was certainly noticeable during the lead up to the 2012 Olympic Games.

BT was an *official communications service partner* for the London 2012 Olympic Games.

Campaign message*: 'BT. Bringing it all together for London 2012.'*

Vauxhall Vivaro, BT Payphones van © J. Chenery (2013).

BT's special 2012 wraparound vehicle branding was first shown outside City Hall, London in September 2008. Initially, 50 BT Payphones vehicles were updated with the new corporate logo, as well as approximately 240 London taxis. Vehicle rebranding was completed by Stewart Signs.

During a key 2012 launch event at the BT Tower, a number of freshly wrapped London taxis were paid to circle around so that attendees would subtly be impressed as they arrived and left.

Openreach vans simply used the 2012 logo, but with another descriptive strapline:
'official telecommunications infrastructure provider'
Note that Openreach lettering had always been purple.

BT wi-fi

In June 2012 BT rebranded its wireless connectivity products, BT Fon, and BT Openzone into a single BT wi-fi brand. Early representations were a white font against a rippled purple background of concentric circles.

BT Sport 2013

BT Sport channels launched on 1 August 2013. The studios were based at the former International Broadcast Centre (now *Here East*) at the Queen Elizabeth Olympic Park, Stratford, London. RedBee Media [www.redbeecreative.com] developed branding that could be used on screen. Advertising agency Abbott Mead Vickers BBDO worked with Stewart Signs who used *3M^{TM} Envision* wrapping film to create the specially liveried vehicles.

BT Sport
GREAT SPORT HAPPENS HERE

Free with BT Broadband

Above: Vauxhall Vivaro in all-blue BT Sport livery © J. Chenery (2013).

168 BT vans were re-branded in the blue wrap. New white van deliveries from 2015 had the logo and waves.

Right: Fiat Doblò in the later BT Sport design © J. Chenery (2015).

Red Bee Media:
"The logo mixes the BT Connected World brand imagery with a font developed specifically for the new brand. Contained in a black lozenge shape, the left-hand corner features the traditional corporate BT font, with partial elements of the globe in red, yellow, lilac, purple and green."

BT Purple

The BT brand was always evolving with new campaigns, colours, and straplines, gaining attention, and market share, with the help of top advertising, and creative design agencies.

The *'Be There'* campaign used purple branding with the 'connected world' logo from 4 August 2017 onwards.

Agency: AMV BBDO. Client: BT with Red & White studio. Aug 2017: "BT is unifying its consumer-facing and B2B brands, including its sport and entertainment offerings, under a singular strapline **'Be There'**, which underlines the role communication plays in people's lives."

[Left: Scan from mailer envelope.]

The Post Office Vehicle Club reported that Nov 2017 was the first sighting of a purple wrapped, branded BT van.

The *'Get in touch bt.com'* message was retained on this livery.

BT purple/blue liveried VW van © J. Chenery (2020).

The development of corporate brand and identity was crucial to BT Group to maintain a strong image in the ever more competitive marketplace. During 2016 it was already looking forward to its next transformation. Elsewhere in the Group, Openreach Ltd was incorporated as a separate company in 2017, due to increasing regulatory pressure on BT, to serve all CPs (Communication Providers) equally and without any implied priority to BT.

Styling the Post Office

British Telecom Centre (BTC)

On the site of the GPO's Central Telegraph Office, the new British Telecom Centre, the company's flagship London building opened in 1985 and finally closed in December 2021.

BTC at 81 Newgate Street © J. Chenery (2017).

The area around St. Paul's was once known as the Post Office District because the nearby buildings were all part of the GPO's hierarchy. Thus GPO North, South, East, West, and the King Edward Building were all once within easy walking distance. GPO West was the Central Telegraph Office (CTO) site.

BT HQ

BT sold its outmoded central London head office in 2019 for £210M in favour of a development at Aldgate East.

Right: BT's new HQ at One Braham, Aldgate East opened November 2021 © J. Chenery 2022. The new registered address is One Braham, Braham Street, London, E1 8EE.

BT Cellnet

BT had previously sold its own mobile business Cellnet/O2 to Telefonica in 2016.

17: BT Comes Full Circle

Twenty-sixteen was a significant year for BT Group as it purchased mobile operator EE in January. The further separation of Openreach was scheduled for March 2017. And BT registered a circle logo* in September 2016, but with all these brands to consider, implementation of new identities could not be rushed.
[In 2022, BT, EE, Plusnet, and Openreach are all separate brands.]
*A circle with transitioning colours with BT in the middle in a simple sans-serif font.

BT Sub-brands

From 2003 when the *connected world* logo was adopted as the one symbol for BT, the sub-brand logos had multiplied into a plethora of varying designs. Wolff Olin's hadn't conceived the one-time *Openworld globe* to be used company wide. The world since had moved on!

Image: Sample of BT brandmarks.

BT needed a more clearly defined brand mark that would be simple to use across all forms of media. *Red&White* design studio developed the BT circle concept, and the refreshed brand was announced in May 2019. Paul Franklin of *Red&White* explained the ethos behind the new logo:

"Because it's BT and everyone knows who they are, we knew that we could have the confidence to make it really simple, and it would still ring true."

The core colour is now purple...

Styling the Post Office

BT Purple

The continued use of purple in the new BT logo gave continuity, whilst showing that the brand was evolving with company values.

Saatchi & Saatchi's *Beyond Limits* campaign launched the new BT brand on 18 October 2019. It was 50 years (01/10/1969) since the Post Office/BT had ceased to be a government department.

Dalton Maag's *BT Font* was retained with added weights. Dalton Maag's London-based typeface design studio was founded in 1991.

Red&White: *"Some people looked at it [the brand] and said, '**It took four years to do a logo that's two letters and a circle?**' But really, it takes four years to go around a business of that size, and to make sure everyone's happy and comfortable with it, and to show why it's right for them."*

Purple Fleet

VW Transporter van with purple BT wrap and circle logo © J. Chenery (2021).

Minimal logo changes were required on BT's purple fleet of vans.

The earlier *'Get in touch bt.com'* markings were removed because the brand is so well-known.

Richard Lloyd, Director of Brand Identity & Design, BT Group plc: *"Red&White worked tirelessly across our entire organisation, guiding us and challenging us, to create a strong and consistent brand that will work brilliantly for everything we do."*

BT Comes Full Circle

BT has described the rational for its fleet liveries as:
'Small vans, and Emergency response vehicles – indigo logo on a white background.
Medium/large vans – indigo livery with the portal, and logo in white.
Electric trial vehicle – white logo and typography on a gradient background.'

White Fleet

BT Group vehicles which were not fully branded as Openreach, or in BT purple, were seen simply marked with the BT Circle.

BT's previously in-house *Fleet Solutions* (vehicle management) was sold to Aurelius Group in September 2019 and rebranded as *Rivus Fleet Solutions*.

Left: White BT Fiat Doblò van © David Whittaker (2020).

BT Broadband

BT's purple branding extended to its *Halo* and *Hybrid Connect* broadband products which included a mobile back-up hub, as fallback in the event of landline (PSTN) failure. With the PSTN (Public Switched Telephone Network) closure scheduled for 2025, the new norm will be to have broadband service as standard, and telephony will only be provided via VOIP (Voice Over Internet Protocol) as an extra, if requested.

TV Marketing

Through the decades, BT's contracted agents made sure its targeted advertising kept it 'on trend' to appeal to growth markets, particularly younger and working audiences. BT's *Beyond Limits* TV ads frequently included an instrumental sample (chorus) from Billie Eilish's song *Bad Guy* (March 2019). Working with renowned partners Saatchi & Saatchi, another advert (Sept 2020) showed an embarrassed 'Pixelated Paula' (as named by her colleague Stuart) whose broadband/wi-fi failed during an important video-linked team meeting. Poor Paula should have chosen BT as her provider! It was no longer a given that BT would always be the consumer's first choice for service.

Styling the Post Office

EE
Everything Everywhere is the name of the mobile network operator that was founded as a JV between *Deutsche Telekom* and *France Telecom* on 1 April 2010. It was rebranded as simply *EE* in October 2012.

BT purchased EE Ltd in January 2016 and currently operates it as a separate brand within BT Group.

Left: EE/BT Phoneshop at Aldgate East

© J. Chenery (2022).

BT Group
On 27 April 2022 BT announced that its consumer operations would focus on the EE brand rather than using the BT name, which would become synonymous with its business market.

"BT Group is getting a makeover so we can speak clearly as one business representing all our brands"

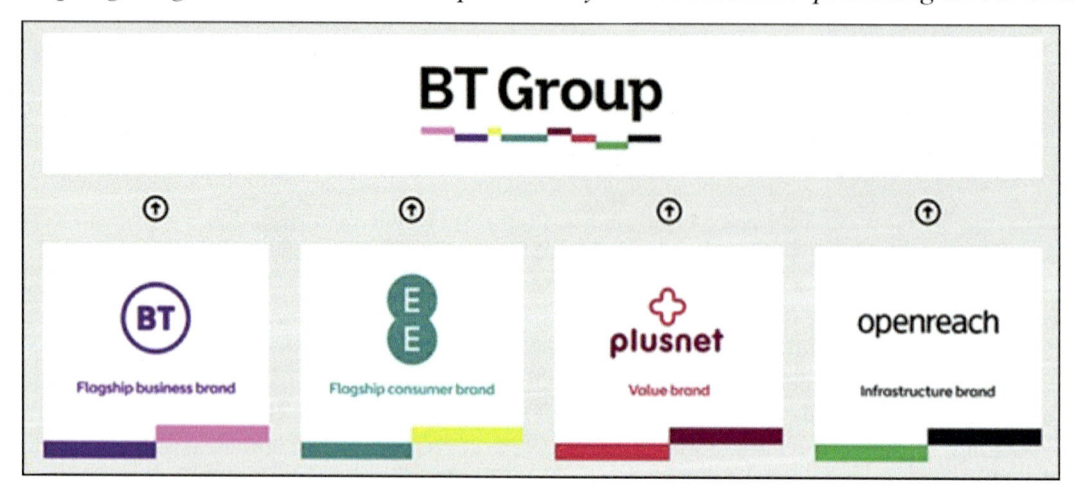

The BT Group hierarchy [from www.bt.com/about/bt/our-brands - viewed 22 September 2022].
BT: Flagship business brand; EE: Flagship consumer brand; plusnet: value brand; openreach: infrastructure brand.

18: Openreach

A brand-new style appeared when Openreach was launched by BT on 11 January 2006. This was a distinctive new wordmark, but to show provenance, the BT *Connected world* globe branding was carried forward to the strapline confirming that Openreach was 'a BT Group business.'

Vauxhall Vivaro van in Openreach livery © J. Chenery (2012).

"Openreach was established in 2006 following an agreement between BT and the UK's telecoms regulator, Ofcom, to implement certain undertakings, pursuant to the Enterprise Act 2002, to ensure that rival telecom operators have equality of access to BT's local network."

Nicknamed the ribbon, the 2006 vehicle livery comprised of six wavy coloured cords which represented telephone lines. The purple wordmark lettering was carried forward to Openreach's website.

Superfast Fibre 2011

In 2011, long-standing BT partner, Westhill Communications first devised a 'brand refresh' for Openreach's vans to highlight the 'Super-fast fibre' rollout programme. Stewart Signs provided the expertise for the vinyl wrap of the vehicles using Scotchprint Graphics.

Left: Superfast fibre Ford Transit 100T300 (2013) LC62 YSS © J. Chenery (2015).

Rear end van markings were introduced to comply with Chapter 8 of *Traffic Signs Manual* (2009) for vehicles undertaking road works or other temporary situations.

By now the original ribbon design has given way to something resembling more of a datastream of flowing multiple colours.

Top and bottom sections of the rear doors display red and yellow chevrons (introduced progressively from 2009) to aid safe working when parked-up on the roadside.

Left: Super fast fibre Fiat Ducato 35 Multijet WM17 LCC (2017) © J. Chenery (2018).

Openreach

Expect Openreach

In August 2013, the buzzword was *"Expect Openreach"* because its engineers work for over 500 Service Providers (SPs) who in turn sell telephone, broadband and TV services to the end users (customers). By 2021, over 660 SPs were supported.

"Our role at Openreach is to keep you connected to your provider. So, when you order a new service, or have a problem with your connection, contact your provider, but expect Openreach!"
[Source: 'Openreach Explained' *YouTube*.]

During 2017 Openreach became a limited company and consequently chose Kelvin House, 123 Judd Street, London WC1H 9NP as its registered address.

Kelvin House, once known as *Trunk Control North* originally housed the Speaking Clock (TIM) and Recorded Information Services (RIS).

Left: Openreach HQ © J. Chenery (2019).

Despite best efforts, to escape its heritage, tentative reminders of the GPO (General Post Office) linger on.

A *'BT Group Business'* strapline was removed in accordance with Ofcom requirements.

Right: Vauxhall Vivaro FL16 GPO
© J. Chenery (2018).

Smart TV 2013

In October 2013, Westhill Communications and Stewart Signs devised a new look livery for Openreach to mark the 'Smart TV revolution' and raise awareness of TV services delivered by fibre Broadband, either FTTP or FTTC. This coincided with the delivery of the first batch of Fiat Doblò Maxi vans.

"Superfast fibre:

Hummingbird: No more humdrum TV.
Astronaut: Stellar TV on demand.
Dinosaur: For TV services with bite."

Superfast fibre is delivered via
FTTC – Fibre To The Cabinet,
or
FTTP – Fibre To The Premises.

The final drop can be either overhead or underground.

Fiat Doblò vans in Dinosaur, Hummingbird, and Astronaut liveries © J. Chenery.

Connecting Communities 2014

Connecting Communities Fiat *Doblò* © J. Chenery (March 2017).

The Superfast fibre campaigns mostly displaced the prominent Openreach wording on van sides. In this instance above, an additional message of 'Connecting Communities' is featured. Rear door wording qualified further with:

"Connecting your community to phone, broadband and TV services." Or *"Connecting the Nation to Phone, Broadband and TV services."*

Electric Vehicles (EVs)

Trials of electric vehicles date back to the Post Office Telecommunications era.

Left: Ford Transit 350 (2011) NK11 DVW on show at Milton Keynes Museum rally © J. Chenery (2014).

Below: Improved battery technology has made reliable production versions of popular vehicles feasible.

Right: A Vauxhall Vivaro-E 3100 Dynamic DS70 YOG on a routine customer visit © R. Haydon (2022).

A green flash sticker states *'Zero emissions 100% Electric Van.'*

Note the special *'fibre optic green* lines doodles' livery which matches Openreach's website presence.

Openreach 2017

On 24 March 2017 Openreach Ltd was incorporated as a separate company, although it was still owned by BT Group. On 11 July, the new livery was revealed. The demarcation from BT was to satisfy OFCOM that Openreach would treat all Communication Providers (CPs) equally. The refreshed branding excluded any reference to BT.

Openreach Vauxhall Combo van "Connecting you to your network" © J. Chenery (2019).

The *Red&White* design studio developed the updated identity which was applied to new vans. For the existing fleet, the strapline and vignette vinyl 'a *BT Group business*' was simply removed.

Openreach: *"The rebrand is a visual demonstration to our CPs and consumers that we're committed to delivering the highest standards to everyone. By 14 July 2020, we completed the rebrand of our vans, buildings, uniforms, and equipment ahead of the original schedule (April 2021) that we'd agreed with Ofcom."*

Styling the Post Office

Understanding Openreach
The Openreach logo/name is essentially Tahoma font that has accentuated styling, noticeably curves at the bottom of the n and h. Typefaces used are typically *openreach medium*, and *openreach bold*. As once with *Post Office Telecommunications*, corporates prefer customised typefaces. Although not a new phrase, *'connecting you to your network'* has now replaced *'a BT Group business'* as the official strapline, giving a consistent message.

Openreach (2019)
Pollitt and Partners (P & P) further revised the Openreach identity with the brief to evolve the brand away from any previous correlation to BT. A colour pallet of *Fibre Violet, Optic Green, Earth Grey*, and a lighter *Live Grey* was considered. Some of these colours and doodles artwork, with map, are featured on the electric vans. EVs with the new livery were first displayed at *ExCel London* in June 2019.

Leading creatives were contracted via P & P, and Wunderman to work their magic on the all-embracing project. Of note were Julie Donfrancesco and Brett Kellett. Julie, who is now freelance refreshed the corporate voice. Here's her narrative of the development:

We're in the business of connecting people, so how we sound matters.	Some of Julie's development work for Openreach from juliesbook.com

Recruitment advert

Become an Openreach engineer and keep Britain talking, creating, sharing, connecting, working, streaming, snapping, playing, filming, swiping, meeting, watching, recording, singing, rapping, speaking, chatting, growing, and … you get the picture.

We're recruiting now
Link to the free wi-fi and apply now at openreach.co.uk/trainee

openreach

"Openreach is the UK's largest broadband provider, looking after millions of kilometres of cable that connects us, every day. This newly independent subsidiary of BT needed a new focus, tone of voice and a brand new set of guidelines to show them exactly how they could tell their story in an open, accessible way. As part of my work with P&P, I wrote this for them across guidelines, recruitment adverts, for internal campaigns, CEO speeches and in films you can even enjoy on the internet - if FTTP floats that particular boat." Julie Donfrancesco.

Openreach

Graphic Doodles

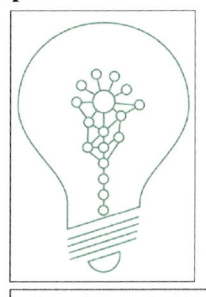

Brett, a graphic designer, and illustrator produced attention-grabbing doodles; line drawings with predominantly green or violet outlines, which represented the fibre lines of the openreach network.

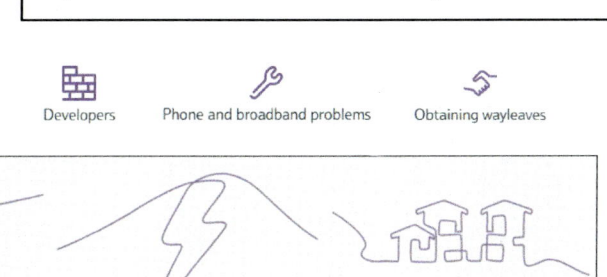

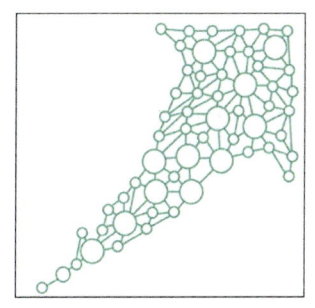

Doodles representing network connectivity, drawn in 'Fibre Violet' and 'Optic Green.'

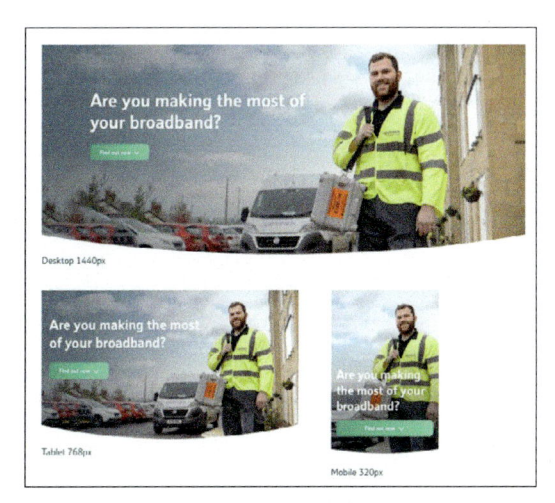

These themes were carried across to Openreach's website(s) with the expertise of UI (User Interface), digital designer Jennie Clark who produced templates allowing hundreds of pages to be consistently built with *Openreach green*, and a darker teal than previously used.

Left: Jennie demonstrates the challenges of the digital world where web page images and text may align and look entirely different, dependent upon users viewing platforms. The examples given are of desktops, tablets, or mobile devices.

Are you making the most of your broadband?

Brand agency Pollitt and Partners was founded in 1987. WPP merged its Wunderman and J Walter Thompson agencies in 2019 to become Wunderman Thompson.

Styling the Post Office

Post Office Tower under construction

The Post Office Tower displaying L I N D the name of main contractors Peter Lind & Co. Ltd.

Post Office Tower under construction © John Hayes (c1963).

Post Office Tower under construction. Colour photos © John Hayes (c1963).

Below:
Why a Post Office Tower?
Exhibition:
March 17-24, 1964, except Sunday.

Left: Why a Post Office Tower exhibition (April 1964) courtesy of BT Group Archives. Ref: TCB 473/P 8986.

19: Post Office Tower

The Post Office Tower was to become the most iconic, and well-known representation of the Post Office's (and later BT's) telecommunications business. This status continues today.

Operationally opened on 8 October 1965 the GPO's radio tower at Museum telephone exchange was officially designated as the Post Office Tower. Photos of the entrance in Maple Street are rare, but this nighttime shot shows an illuminated sign, white lettering on a red background. In bygone days, the front entrance extended far down the side of Cleveland Mews forming a large open, elevated platform along which the massing crowds of visitors could be managed.

The tower created a unique brand; originally it was superfluous to have lettering around the top; it was the tallest building in Great Britain, and everyone knew the landmark. This changed as competing developments in London designed ever higher skyscrapers, some with prominent business names. After privatisation in 1984 the new trading name BRITISH TELECOM was displayed at the top of the former Post Office Tower.

Booklet: The Post Office Tower London PH1676 12/70 designed by Banks and Miles, photography by Mike Peters. Image courtesy of BT Group Archives. Ref: TCB 346/T 841.

The Plaque

Right: 8 October 1965 Harold Wilson declares the Tower open, watched by Postmaster-General Tony Benn and Clement Attlee a former PMG.

Photo courtesy of BT Group Archives. Ref: TCB 477/08-10-65.

Left: Post Office Tower plaque on display in BT Group Archives © J. Chenery (2018).

David Walton writes: *"The Tower is anchored to the Howland Street building (Museum exchange) at T4*. When you came out of the lift at T4 there was a VIP lounge and cinema. The plaque was fitted to the side wall of the balcony that overlooked the yard."*

[*A7 bridge deck POEEJ Vol 55, p74.]

Postmaster-General Tony Benn:

"...when people saw the Post Office Tower, and particularly when they were able to go up it, there was a huge pride in that achievement."

Post Office Tower

Tony Benn on Stuart Maconie's TV Towns 2007

"…the public built this with their (taxpayers) money…when we bought a stamp or paid to make a telephone call. [As a public building], the people felt it belonged to them."

Topofthetower (Butlin's concession)

The topofthetower restaurant operated by Butlins Holidays cleverly had a cogwheel symbol logo (red on blue) which represented the drive wheel for the revolving 34th floor restaurant.

The cogwheel-patterned branded carpet of the revolving 34th floor. The diagonal line is the split between the stationary and moving sections.

The cogwheel branding was extended to menus and serviettes. The topofthetower staff wore complimentary blue jackets with red trim.

The Post Office Tower Stamps were designed by former Wimbledon Art School student, 32-years old Clive Abbott (1933-2008). He had previously designed greetings telegrams for the GPO.

Issued in values of 3d and 1/3 (pre-decimal money.)

Scan from author's collection: Souvenir presentation pack of Post Office Tower stamps.

Styling the Post Office

Banks and Miles

John Banks from *Banks and Miles* (ex-PO/BT design agency) interview with Matthew Standage 1 April 2014.

"One of things we wanted so much to do, I am very glad they didn't let us: we said, 'Why don't you put the Post Office Tower in three-dimensional lettering all around the top?' Of course, it became telecom tower soon after that."

The LED Infoband

In 1985 the first static yellow BRITISH TELECOM signs spanned floors 36 and 37 of the tower. These were replaced by BT Pipers in 1991.

Ben Verwaayen, BT CEO (2003-2008) *"The BT Tower is one of the most visible representations of the BT brand."*

In 2004 the signage panels were extended to a full 360 degrees. The three back-lit BT signs were enhanced with the seven changing colours of the *Connected World* logo continuously projected around the top, giving a sense of movement. By 2009, technology allowed installation of a wraparound LED panel 'a giant electronic information band' which could display messages as well as the BT brand. Circa 2017 a major upgrade of the LED panels, control gear, and software (arranged by Kronman Associates) allowed greater control of individual pixels, colour, and contrast, enhancing, and maintaining the integrity of the BT brand.

BT's Karen Ahern: *"We're hugely proud of the Tower's new LED infoband."*

The LED panels had no problem displaying the revised (2019) BT logo and updated colours (as pictured.)

BT Tower showing the infoband around the top floors 36 and 37 © J. Chenery (2022).

References and End Notes

20: References and End Notes

Notwithstanding the author's own collection, and images from official archives, it would not have been possible to convey the 'style of the Post Office' without the contributions from the photographers gratefully listed below.

Photographs sourced from these contributors either directly or via Creative Commons licences:
Adam Oliver, Andrew Emmerson, Andy Cole, Brian Forode, Chris Downer (photos and handstamps), Dave Bullock, Dave Collier, David Cott, David Whittaker, Jason Cross, John and Mike Hayes, John Murdoch, Jim Osley, KP Simpson, Laurence Rudolf, Lynda Bullock, Malcolm Jones, Mark Skillen, Mike Ashworth, Mike Street, Nick Skinner, Nigel Turner, Paul David Smith, Richard Haydon, Simon Chappell, Simon Cowper-Smith, Steve Jones, Wallace Henning. And via Flickr: *Jelm6, Post Box, Saxonessex, and Sludge G.*

Special thanks to Christopher Hogan of the Post Office Vehicle Club who assisted with the historical accuracy and kept the publication on track. Also, to Mike Street for allowing use of his photographs.

Archive material and photos from The Postal Museum, and BT Group Archives; additional photos from the Banks and Miles Archive, Lettering, Printing and Graphic Design collections, Department of Typography & Graphic Communication, University of Reading. Thanks to the teams at The Postal Museum, and BT Group Archives for access to files, and for their professionalism.
Other contributions and help from Andrew Emmerson, Adam Oliver, Sarah Stevens, Simon Marshall (Head of Brand POL), Julie Donfrancesco, Brett Kellett, David Walton, Nick Job, John Tythe, Bob Fastner, and Tom Peake.

This book was inspired by the article in *Post Horn* (magazine of the Post Office Vehicle Club) 17/107, entitled *Post Office Design* by Christopher Hogan. Also, by the dissertation (2014) of Matthew Standage -*The Post Office corporate identity 1965-1980,* and *Death by a thousand cuts: a brief note on a lost opportunity for a new General Post Office logo* by David Cabianca.

All of the vehicles mentioned and illustrated in this book are recorded by the Post Office Vehicle Club which is the leading resource for historical Post Office postal and telecommunication fleet studies: povehclub.org.uk

Other References
The British Phonebox by Nigel Linge and Andy Sutton.
Built for Service: Post Office Architecture by Julian Osley.
Old Letter Boxes by Martin Robinson.

Styling the Post Office

Post Office Magazines, and Journals.
Telephone Boxes by Gavin Stamp.
Telephone Boxes by Neil Johannessen.
Viewdata in Action – a comparative study of Prestel by Rex Winsbury.

Selected web resources used
British Post Office Architects: britishpostofficearchitects.weebly.com
British Telephones: britishtelephones.com
BT Digital Archives: bt.com/btdigitalarchives
Flickr: flickr.com and Geograph: geograph.org.uk
Great Britain Philatelic Society: gbps.org.uk
Machorne.wordpress.com/2020/02/24/trafalgar-square-post-office-gone-but-not-forgotten/
The Postal Museum: postalmuseum.org
Sam's Telecomms Index: samhallas.co.uk/telecomms.htm
Simon's Interests: transconnect.co.uk
Telecommunications Heritage Group: thg.org.uk and Resource at thgr.co.uk
Wikipedia: en.wikipedia.org

Cover Illustrations
All © J. Chenery 2009-2022.

Front: Royal Mail Vauxhall Vivaro KR59 JHZ outside BT's Baynard House, Blackfriars, London. A KX + *Coins & Cards* telephone kiosk stands adjacent (2017).

Rear: A Mid-Bronze Green MAX 12 mobile telephone exchange is parked next to K6 and K8 Currant Red telephone kiosks at Milton Keynes Museum (2014).
A *CLICK. DROP. DONE.* DAF artic Royal Mail trailer PJ16 YTN, PRDC (Princess Royal Distribution Centre) running number VOC84 is being driven into the (new) underground parking complex at Mount Pleasant sorting office, London (2022).
A BT Payphones Vauxhall Vivaro FD06 CFK finished in *Olympics 2012* livery is parked at BT Brentwood (2009).
 Two double aperture EIIR pillar boxes (Machan Engineering, Scotland), together with a *Business Box* (franked mail only), outside a Post Office branch of WH Smith (2019).
A line up of preserved/restored telecommunication and postal vehicles at a rally at Milton Keynes Museum (2015).

References and End Notes

End Notes
Design in the Post Office encompassed so many different aspects, and to mention all of them in a single book has limitations. To end this edition is a brief look at the 1968 square-shaped pillar box, and modern-day delivery methods.

Type F Pillar Box 1968

Henrion's mid-1960s aspirations for a complete *House Style* for the Post Office conveniently manifested in the first rectangular-shaped pillar box (long in development) of the twentieth century. It may have been a good pairing with the (then new) K8 telephone kiosk in a modern town centre setting. Anticipated to also be finished in *House Style* red (539), this too was not initially the case, and red 538 prevailed for a while.

The double aperture *Type F* pillar box, which was designed by David Mellor (industrial engineer), and manufactured by Vandyke Engineering Ltd. in 1968. The sheet steel fabricated box did not weather well. The raised lettering of the crown and cypher was evidence of replacement plates on the exterior doors, due to excessive rusting! By 1974 this design was superseded by the *Type G* cast rectangular iron box.

David Mellor: *"I think it is quite attractive and blends well into the mood of the sixties."* [Post Office Magazine Feb 1966.]

Above: The Type F box seen at Debden postal store © J. Chenery (2012).
Left: A blanking/locking plate for pillar box apertures when taken out of use. This one used the Banks and Miles' double line typeface. © W. Henning.

Styling the Post Office

Royal Mail Style

Modern Delivery Methods (DMs) use a combination of satchels, trolleys (LWTs and HCTs) and shared vans.

Left: A postman delivers door to door using his satchel/postbag (2022).

Centre: A hi-top Fiat Doblò WR63 GPZ serial 3050902 (2014).

Top right: Vans collect post from pillar boxes and drop off loaded HCTs (High Capacity Trolleys) for the postman/woman to walk extended delivery areas (2018).

Left: Typically, for walks that are within a mile of the DO (Delivery Office) the HCTs are solely used (2020).

Photos © J. Chenery (2014-2022).